Animal Firm: A Corporation Acquires Animal Farm

EDWARD A. LOUCKS

DEDICATED TO MY FRIEND AND MENTOR,
JOHN H. SUPPLEE, WHO HAS TRIED FOR
MOST OF HIS CAREER TO HELP ME ACT AND
THINK LIKE A BUSINESSMAN.

TABLE OF CONTENTS

Table of Contents

PREFACE

AS WORLD WAR II CAME TO A CLOSE, British author George Orwell published *Animal Farm*, a satirical look at totalitarian government. When we think of the adjective "totalitarian," what pops onto the mental monitor is a picture of Hitler or Stalin, or more recently, Saddam Hussein or Muammar Gadafi. We think of bad people in places of great power and influence—bad because they take away the rights and liberties we in the democratic West take for granted as being God-given and inalienable. They are also bad because they oppose us good people and our policies pertaining to them.

A more useful definition of "totalitarian" is "any entity which demands our ultimate loyalty." That entity, whether political, economic, educational, nonprofit or religious, tolerates no higher claim to our submission, our obedience, our loyal adulation—not God or religious belief, not family, not ethical convictions, no philosophical system. Nothing can be appealed to as a counter-argument to a demand by the totalitarian agency.

To be a member in good standing, to enjoy the benefits of that association, and to hope and expect to advance in such an organization, one must submit to its values, its leadership, and its rules. When a person claims that a higher authority exists, he or she is a marked person and his or her effectiveness in that place is finished. The next step is for that person to be excluded from key decision making councils, loss of influence, shunning, even expulsion. In some of the more rabid or fundamentalist organizations, disloyalty can result in formally sanctioned execution.

Orwell sneered at the proclaimed ideals of the classless society. Such claims are specious, he wrote, because the ideals soon become polluted by a group of activists seeking privilege, and once finding it, building a fortress around it. The inevitable new hierarchy of privilege becomes, in a totalitarian community, permanent, and great effort is taken to justify its permanence. He saw what was happening in the highly stratified "classless" societies toiling under the red flag of Communism, with their bureaucracies made up of people who, like Orwell's ruling class of Pigs, announced that "all animals are equal, but some are more equal than others."

In Western democracies, with their varieties of representational systems, checks and balances, and free speech and press, there appear to be some protections against totalitarianism, protecting those dwelling therein so they can enjoy a modicum of comfort. But totalitarianism, wherever it appears, is totalitarianism nonetheless. And when a person in charge of an organization has the power to tell another how to dress, how and when to speak, where to park the car, when and where to eat lunch, when days away from the organization are permissible, including days set aside by that person for religious observances or family activities, that person is a dictator, and the line between dictatorship and totalitarianism is a narrow one indeed. A benevolent dictator is still a dictator, and the freedoms of those dwelling in the turf of a benevolent dictator are just as diminished as those under any other brand.

This is the price one pays, even in a democracy, for membership in good standing in almost any organization, or subunit within that organization. A person joins such organizations as a matter of free choice, and can usually leave such entities the same way by freely choosing to walk away, provided the organization is not a fanatical society possessing secrets it must guard. Such organizations as organized crime syndicates, a fundamentalist sect of any religion, or a gang of street thugs, are totalitarian entities, possessing the self-claimed right to protect their secrets from outsiders, even at the cost of the life of the miscreant.

For most people, in most organizations, the freedom to walk away generally has a high economic price. The price to stay in such an organization is paid in lost self-esteem, of desired freedoms, of self-respect, and of the right to pursue happiness, however that is defined. It certainly leads quickly to the loss of a steady income, benefits, and the prestige of carrying a business card with a widely recognized logo of an admired and well-known organization.

Orwell attacks big, totalitarian states. Our great danger today comes from millions of relatively small organizations or subunits within an organization. An organization is *any group of two or more individuals who voluntarily choose to surrender their absolute freedom to a greater whole in order to achieve a commonly held or agreed upon objective or aspiration.*

The organization soon needs additional resources and must go forth to recruit others, not always fully and candidly informing them of the total cost of membership. Those who advance in the organizational hierarchy are sometimes the most able ones, the most creative ones, the ones with the best leadership skills, the most trustworthy ones, but more often they are the most fear-driven, the most control-oriented, the most psychologically insecure, the most spiritually malnourished. The chaos of creativity terrifies them. They are suspicious of nonconformists. They take themselves seriously and are uncomfortable with those who indulge in self-deprecating humor. Risk, as a recent book title reminds us, is a four-letter word. They are only content in an environment in which "everything is under control"—theirs.

To advance in today's organization, one must also be focused on short-term, quantifiable results. They are not rewarded for building the organization of the future by spending time and money on growing future leadership for the firm—only those quantifiable items that appear in the quarterly profit-and-loss statement matter. If a person wants to get ahead in an organization, or maybe even just to survive, he or she must not look too far ahead.

Brilliant, if occasionally ruthless, entrepreneurs created our country's industrial might. They prospered in the second half of the nineteenth century.

Early in the twentieth century, as these geniuses died off, they were some-times replaced by capable descendants. More often, however, they were replaced by hired managers, professionals—mercenaries who advanced to the foot of the throne through cautious maneuvering and a talent for sur-vival that would make a cockroach jealous. They did not possess the grand vision of the entrepreneurs nor the social conscience that led many of those "robber barons" to endow huge foundations dedicated to educational and charitable purposes. All they sought was to manage the machine for a few more years, to enjoy the prestige and perquisites of power and the comfort of control, and to ensure a comfortable retirement for themselves and their families.

These mercenaries—professional soldiers—used metaphors of vio-lence in their descriptions of the world of commerce. "We are at war with the competition!" "It's a jungle out there!" "This is not the place for the weak-kneed, the thin-skinned, or the tender-minded." And so forth. Competition is what brings out the best in people. Cooperation and collaboration has no place in this dog-eat-dog world. And sometimes one has to bend the rules of morality to live to play another day.

A commonly held metaphor is that of the organization as a *machine*, with the CEO operating it from the outside. The CEO is not part of the ma-chine, which is essentially a lifeless collection of replaceable parts, cleverly assembled by the best human brains available for the purpose of producing something desired by consumers. The function of the CEO is to keep the machine running at top optimal speed, to diagnose the problem when it is not performing up to expectations, to remove and replace the inoperative expendable part when necessary, and get the machine back to production as quickly as possible. The "expendable, replaceable parts" are frequently human beings, who are regarded as "overhead," to be kept at a minimum number and the lowest possible pay rate to "control" costs.

The CEO occasionally needs help to keep the machine running, so a staff of highly paid executives is hired—accountants, corporate attorneys, sales and marketing people, human resources professionals, and information systems technicians. These highly paid people are also "outside of the machine," not part of the line operation, not directly or tangibly producing saleable goods.

The alternative metaphor, that has gained attention recently in the fields of quantum physics and biology but is as yet under-appreciated in organizational life, is that of a *living system*. A tree, for example, is a living system. One can plant a tree, water and fertilize it, prune it, pick its fruit, even graft branches into its trunk, but he or she cannot turn the tree from one kind into another, force it to grow faster or in a different climate, or alter the tree in any radical way without seriously damaging or destroying it. The tree has a life of its own, and humans can do little to change the laws of nature with regard to the tree. An obvious reason why the living system metaphor has not caught on quickly in organizations is that a living system is not readily subject to human control. So the mechanistic view prevails over the organic, even though the very name "organization" calls us to think differently.

Another example, perhaps more clearly related to the life of an organization, is the human body. We humans are living systems. We can do more and more things to the human body, thanks to modern science and medicine, but we pay a high price when we do so.

Think of the business organization as a living system. The brain could represent the executive staff, including the CEO. They make the decisions and give direction to the other parts of the body. But—and this is critical—they are still *part of the body*. They are not outside the body, as in the machine metaphor, and each decision they make not only affects the body but themselves as well.

Furthermore, the brain, without the body, is useless. We've all seen the films with mad scientists storing brains in vats of formaldehyde, awaiting the right body for implantation. As long as the brain is separated from the body, it just sits in the bottle soaking up the chemicals.

Other parts of the body work together to make the whole body functional. The legs for running and walking, the arms for lifting and embracing, the abdomen for enclosing and protecting the vital organs that give the body its viability. In the corporation, the legs could be sales and marketing; the arms, manufacturing, production and distribution; the heart and lungs research and development—you create representations that more adequately fit your organization.

There is one representation that is common to most organizations—the digestive tract, from mouth to anus. This is the human resources department. It brings nutrients (new employees) into the corporation through the mouth after careful selection, prepares them by the digestive process (orientation and training) for duties and functions at various locations in the body (as red or white corpuscles). The "misfits" are processed through the intestinal tract for elimination at the teminus of the digestive tract.

If unhealthy food is ingested, or too much food, or both, the body gets fat. There are two ways to lose weight; change the diet while increasing exercise, or, amputation. Amputation produces drastic side effects from which the body may never fully recover. Even with prosthetic devices, the body never functions as well as it did before. It is used only as a drastic last step to save the rest of the living system from corruption. Changing the diet and increasing the exercise is like adjusting the size of the corporation by hiring freezes and attrition, producing minor inconveniences for the body as a whole. The across-the-board layoff is like an amputation. The whole body goes into shock for a time, and never fully recovers its former grace, confidence, and strength. Layoffs are treated with a shocking casualness in today's organizations—a quick and easy way to make the short-term numbers look good or to prepare the company for an acquisition or merger—or perhaps merely to improve the value of the stock.

The organization, then, is more like a living system than a machine. It has a life of its own over which rational human beings have some influence, but less control than they fancy or desire. And every part of the system is important to the whole, which, when intact, is greater than the sum of its parts.

An elderly woman in my childhood neighborhood used to walk down the street with great effort, requiring the assistance of two canes. I found out indirectly that she had suffered frostbite as a little girl, and eventually had to sacrifice her two pinky toes to the surgeon's knife. As she grew older, it became harder for her to maintain her balance, until as an old woman, she could walk only with the aid of her canes, all because she lost what many of us regard to be a relatively unimportant part of our anatomy.

With recent changes in the organizational environment—globalization, the tremendous impact of technological advances, unprecedented economic chaos, and the growing gap between the rich and the rest of us— we find our lives not more pleasant but more frenzied. We are working harder than ever before without sizable increases in pay, so that our actual hourly earnings have dropped. The competition from other organizations is fierce, and we have to "run faster and faster just to stay in the same place." The disparity of income between the richest and the poorest is not improving anywhere in the world. People are becoming technologically obsolete in their early 50's while medical advances are increasing their longevity, so they can expect to have another 30 years of potential productivity after they are given "early retirement."

Is there a conspiracy behind all this unpleasantness? I agree with Robert Reich who says, No—there is no conspiracy. He writes in *The Future of Success* that our lives are not controlled by an individual or even an oligarchy of individuals— just millions of people making hundreds of decisions an hour, creating unawares the environment in which we must find ways to survive.

Control, then, is an illusion. Chaos is the perceived reality. The Pigs in Orwell's novel had good motives when they started out, but were soon corrupted by the same natural instincts we humans all have. We find our privileges pleasant and do what we have to do to protect and increase them. In organizations, our very personalities seem to change as we climb up the ladder of corporate power, changing us from collaborative team players to command-and-control exploiters. As the majority discover they have been left behind, their personalities change also—from collaborative team players to embittered, passive-aggressive termites chewing at the foundation of the organization.

Altogether, this makes organizational life pretty unpleasant. In the 1930's, Reinhold Niebuhr, a theologian, wrote *Moral Man and Immoral Society*, in which he explained the inevitability of it all. When two people are in relationship, that relationship has the potential of being governed by an ethic of *love*—selfless giving to one another for the other's benefit, with no expectation of return favors. When the two become an organization, the love ethic no longer governs; the best that can be attained in an organization is an ethic based on *justice*—mutual back-scratching, in which the mutuality is regulated by the courts. Niebuhr saw no clear alternative to this, and concluded that life in the organization would never be as pleasant as we would like it to be. Nor would organizations ever be able to achieve actions of high morality—they would always settle at the level of the lowest common denominator. Democracy at best is little more than a process for "finding proximate solutions to insoluble problems."

Do we despair? Is there any hope for pleasantness in our collective life? That is the object of our exploration in this book. I began writing as an exercise in therapy what has evolved into a much longer work than originally imagined, after having been given an early retirement package. A consulting contract, part of the deal, required me to say nothing negative about the company or my boss. Therefore, I will not name the company or any member of it, but I will say it was one of the most unpleasant employment experiences in a long career. Is this where the "new economy" is headed?

One can legitimately wonder if Orwell knew how his book would end when he started it. Likewise, one can wonder what the conclusion of this work will be. I have a premonition, but I hope I change my mind as I progress through the writing.

CHAPTER ONE

The Past is Prologue—Again!

Work is the curse of the drinking classes.
Oscar Wilde

I like work; it fascinates me. I can sit and look at it for hours.
Jerome K. Jerome

MR. JONES, FORMER OWNER of Manor Farm, had been dead for more than 30 years. His wife had given up trying to get the farm back from the animals that had taken it over and renamed it "Animal Farm" so long ago. Her grandson, Charles, had no interest in farming, and had pursued, rather successfully, a career in corporate law.

That all changed one day when the current generation of Pigs approached him about becoming an "investor." Seeing this as an opportunity to regain what was rightfully his by inheritance, Charles put together a consortium of investors and became, on paper at least, the owner of Animal Farm, with the Pigs staying on as paid employees—a most convenient arrangement, since he knew nothing about farming. He regarded it as quite demeaning to dig in real dirt and walk through manure for a living. Any respectable farmer today owned a corporation that amassed vast properties and hired college trained agribusiness grads to run the place. How they did that, and how they treated their employees, was of no concern to the

1

investors, as long as they turned in a good *pee-n-ell* at least three quarters out of every four.

Mr. Jones lost control of Manor Farm because he was not a good manager, not because he was not a good farmer. He knew farming, all right, but he found it tedious and beneath his dignity. He also found his wife boring. In fact, his life in general was a drag, so he took to the solace of alcohol to relieve the boredom. Sometimes he drank at home, but as his wife's complaints increased in frequency and volume, he began to patronize a nearby pub, where he could drink with friends, most of whom were men who were accomplished wife-bashers. They sat there by the hour, moaning and groaning about how little satisfaction they got from being married. They played games of "Can you top this?" to determine who was the most miserable at home.

The pub had several regular female patrons at first, but they gradually gravitated elsewhere, and formed a club of women not interested in the things men found pleasurable—drinking, chewing, spitting, belching, gambling, racing their cars, and chasing after attractive and willing sex objects.

The surroundings and cultural setting Old Man Jones found comfortable disappeared by the time young Charles came along. Times were more prosperous, and women drank with their husbands—not in pubs or bars, but in country clubs, friends' parties, or fancy restaurants. They met with their non-career-oriented female friends for long lunches while their husbands had power lunches with professional colleagues. A man must be able to walk, talk, and do business after a three-martini lunch, or he was not made of the right stuff for the corporate world. Women must look good, be culturally enlightened, smoke dainty cigarettes, and avoid getting sloppy drunk by nursing glasses of white wine rather than distilled products.

This style of living was expensive and required a lot of free time. One had to find a way to make a lot of money without having to work too hard or too long. The best way to do this was to own enough income-producing investments to be able to hire other people to do the work while providing the investor with enough residual income to support the life style he and his family had come to think they deserved and to which they would like to become accustomed.

Investing in "Animal Farm" seemed like a good way to add a brick in the wall protecting Charles from the prospect of insufficiency. The animals had developed some good skills at the agricultural trade by now. The old generation of pioneers had died off and been replaced by a new breed of animals that knew how to work smarter rather than harder.

In the yard between the barn and the house there was a shrine to Old Major, the prize-winning hog who had the dream that resulted in "Animal Farm." Once a year, the animals held a commemoration honoring the Founding Quadrupeds, including a recitation of Old Major's "dream" speech. Youngsters would compete for the honor of reciting from memory the speech Old Major gave three days before he died. It went something like this:

> Comrades, you have heard already about the strange dream that I had last night. But I will come to the dream later. I have something else to say first. I do not think, comrades, that I shall be with you for many months longer, and before I die, I feel it my duty to pass on to you such wisdom as I have acquired. I have had a long life, I have had much time for thought as I lay alone in my stall, and I think I may say that I understand the nature of life on this earth as well as any animal now living. It is about this that I wish to speak to you.
>
> Now, comrades, what is the nature of this life of ours? Let us face it: our lives are miserable, laborious, and short. We are born, we are given just so much food as will keep breath in our bodies, and those of us who are capable of it are forced to work to the last atom of our strength and

the very instant that our usefulness has come to an end we are slaughtered with hideous cruelty. No animal in England knows the meaning of happiness or leisure after he is a year old. No animal in England is free. The life of an animal is misery and slavery: that is the plain truth.

But is this simply a part of the order of nature? Is it because this land of ours is so poor that it cannot afford a decent life to those who dwell upon it? No, comrades, a thousand times no! The soil of England is fertile, its climate is good, it is capable of affording food in abundance to an enormously greater number of animals than now inhabit it. This single farm of ours would support a dozen horses, twenty cows, hundreds of sheep—and all of them living in a comfort and dignity that are now almost beyond our imagining. Why then do we continue in this miserable condition? Because nearly the whole of the produce of our labor is stolen from us by human beings. There, comrades, is the answer to all our problems. It is summed up in a single word—Man. Man is the only real enemy we have. Remove Man from the scene, and the root cause of hunger and overwork is abolished forever.

Man is the only creature that consumes without producing. He does not give milk, he does not lay eggs, he is too weak to pull the plough, he cannot run fast enough to catch rabbits. Yet he is lord of all the animals. He sets them to work, he gives back to them the bare minimum that will prevent them from starving, and the rest he keeps for himself. Our labor tills the soil, our dung fertilizes it, and yet there is not one of us that owns more than his bare skin. You cows that I see before me, how many thousands of gallons of milk have you given during this last year? And what happened to that milk which should have been breeding up sturdy calves? Every drop of it has gone down the throats of our enemies. And you hens, how many eggs have you laid in this last year, and how many of those eggs ever hatched into chickens? The rest have all gone to market to bring in money for Jones and his men. And you, Clover, where are those four foals you bore, who should have been the support and pleasure of your old age? Each was sold at a year old—you will never see one of them again. In return for your four confinements and all your labor in the fields, what have you ever had except your bare rations and a stall?

And even the miserable lives we lead are not allowed to reach their natural span. For myself I do not grumble, for I am one of the lucky ones. I am twelve years old and have had over four hundred children. Such is the natural life of a Pig. But no animal escapes the cruel knife in the end. You young porkers who are sitting in front of me, every one of you will scream your lives out at the block within a year. To that horror we must all come—cows, pigs, hens, sheep, everyone. Even the horses and dogs have no better fate. You, Boxer, the very day that those great muscles of yours lose their power, Jones will sell you to the knacker, who will cut your throat and boil you down for the foxhounds. As for the dogs, when they grow old and toothless, Jones ties a brick round the necks and drowns them in the nearest pond.

Is it not crystal clear, then, comrades, that all the evils of this life of ours spring from the tyranny of human beings? Only get rid of Man, and the produce of our labor will be our own. Almost overnight we would become rich and free. What then must we do? Why work night and day, body and soul, for the overthrow of the human race! That is my message to you, comrades: Rebellion! I do not know when that Rebellion will come, it might be in a week or in a hundred years, but I know, as surely as I see this straw beneath my feet, that sooner or later justice will be done. Fix your eyes on that, comrades, throughout the short remainder of your lives! And above all, pass on this message of mine to those who come after you, so that future generations shall carry on the struggle until it is victorious.

And remember, comrades, your resolution must never falter. No argument must lead you astray. Never listen when they tell you that Man and the animals have a common interest, that the prosperity of the one is the prosperity of the others. It is all lies. Man serves the interest of no creature except himself. And among us animals let there be perfect unity, perfect comradeship in the struggle. All men are enemies. All animals are comrades.

I have little more to say. I merely repeat, remember always your duty of enmity towards Man and all his ways. Whatever goes upon two legs is an enemy. Whatever goes upon four legs, or has wings, is a friend. And remember also that in fighting against Man, we must not come to resemble him. Even when you have conquered him, do not adopt his vices. No animal must ever live in a house, or sleep in a bed, or wear clothes, or drink alcohol, or smoke tobacco, or touch money, or engage in trade. All the habits of Man are evil. And, above all, no animal must ever tyrannize over his own kind. Weak or strong, clever or simple, we are all brothers. No animal must ever kill any other animal. All animals are equal.

The Pigs found the concluding paragraph of the "dream" speech offensive. As soon as their power was consolidated, the Pigs had proceeded to acquire for themselves all the emoluments, privileges and habits Old Major had warned them against, and they were not about to give them up. So, the revised standard version of the speech left the concluding paragraph out completely, and any animal found possessing a copy of the original version was severely punished.

The shrine was built in honor of all the Founding Quadrupeds, not just Old Major, although his statue was largest and most revered. Other statues were erected honoring such heroes as Napoleon the 1st, the first great leader who consolidated the Rebellion and founded Animal Farm. He fought off the humans who tried to retake the Farm. He exposed Snowball, his co-founder, as a traitor, and drove him from the Farm. He thought up the name "Animal Farm" and made the decisions that made the enterprise viable and sustaining. His leadership was firm, sometimes harsh, but he kept the farm working and profitable. He eventually died of too much rich food and drink from the Jones family larder.

Another statue honored Squealer, Napoleon the 1st's propaganda minister, a Pig with a gift for glib gab. This year's winner of the Old Major recitation contest was a descendant of Squealer, carrying on the family tradition of winning battles with the tongue and staying in favor with the powerful through ingratiation and sycophancy. A final statue, the only one not of a Pig, was of Boxer, the lovable, strong, loyal, but not too bright, horse. He kept the farm alive with his brute strength, and was most responsible for the success of one of Napoleon the 1st's early capital construction projects—the windmill. Boxer died of overwork, and was revered as the perfect model of "followership" by all the hourly workers on the Farm. His willingness to work long hours, his cheerful loyalty, and his enthusiastic obedience to every order given by the Pigs was hailed by the Farm's leaders as an example for all when extra effort without extra pay was required—as it was with growing frequency. Boxer was the perfect model of the business axiom: if what you are presently doing does not produce the results you desire, do it harder and faster.

Of course, Boxer's statue was not life-size—that would have made it much bigger than the statues of the Pigs. "All animals are equal, but some are more equal than others."

CHAPTER TWO

The Farm Becomes the Firm

> The only existential meaning of "enterprise" is what business-
> men happen to be doing at the moment, and "free" is merely the
> accompanying demand that they be left alone to do it.
>
> David T. Bazelon
> *The Paper Economy*

THE TRAPPINGS AND TRASH of the 40th anniversary celebration had just barely been gathered up when the word began to leak out that the enterprise was in serious financial trouble. The year was1985. Strangely, one by one, certain animals were becoming conspicuous by their absence, with no one being willing or able to explain their disappearance. Months went by and suspicions grew. The tension was so thick one could inhale it. Finally, the pressure to hold a general meeting so the leadership could answer some questions could no longer be resisted.

The meeting was convened on August 7, 1985. It was held in the barn rather than in the house where the leaders had their offices. All the animals were present, looking hostile. All the leaders were there, looking apprehensive.

Several generations earlier, the Manor Farm, owned by Jones and operated at a reasonable profit until his drinking problem intervened, had been taken over by the animals. It was renamed Animal Farm, and had been run as a relatively prosperous enterprise for four decades. Now, it was suddenly obvious that the apparent prosperity was chimerical—smoke, mirrors, and cooked books.

The meeting was presided over by Napoleon the 13th, a direct descendent of the founder of the Farm. (Most animals were still struggling with Arabic numerals and had not yet approached the idea of using Roman numerals.) The current Napoleon the 13th compensated for lack of intelligence, wisdom or wit with a loud voice and a hyperactive style. He never started a conversation or permitted another to complete a sentence—he only gave orders. No conversation in which he was involved ever lasted more than about 45 seconds. As for the number 13, it was just an estimate that no one chose to question.

As soon as he called for order, the largest animal present, a magnificent horse named Boxer, after his ancestor (horses are strong but not bright, and they didn't use numbers at all) demanded an explanation for the disappearance of several cows recently. The exchange became heated as Napoleon the 13th tried to evade the truth. Boxer persisted, encouraged by the other animals, until Napoleon the 13th was forced to make a grisly admission: "We had to sell them to the butcher in order for the Farm to survive."

There were gasps and loud cries as the animals realized their dear friends had become cash cows. Most visibly upset, though he made little noise, was Emerson, the prize bull who had sired many of the victims. He'd been at the Firm longer than most other four-legged creatures, and as a young bull had won the competition for delivery of Old Major's speech. He was regarded as wise because he didn't say much. His motto: "It takes a darn good word to better a good silence." And, he was wise, indeed—and trusted.

All the other animals came to him with their confidences. They asked him for advice, and he was wise enough not to give them any bull. Instead, he would ask questions until the seeker found the answer on his or her own. When asked a direct question, Emerson always paused until it was absolutely silent and all eyes were on him. This was not so much a requirement of his ego as a habit he had of thinking carefully before saying anything. His responses to questions were invariably short, pithy and memorable. One could hear the unspoken words— "Well, of course!"—breathed by all hearers.

The Pigs were very suspicious of Emerson. They watched him closely. He had too much power, too much influence.

A loud and boisterous series of demands ensued for an alternative method of meeting the financial shortfalls of Animal Farm. "Can you suggest one?" one of the lesser Pigs shouted above the growing roar. "We've been trying for months to come up with one. If you have any ideas, we will certainly take them under advisement."

Few of the animals knew what "under advisement" meant, but all of them were offended by the pomposity of the tone. The Pigs began to make movements toward the house, but they were quickly surrounded by the animals, who by now were getting hysterical.

"Don't even think about leaving this barn until we have a better method for paying our bills than selling us one by one to the butcher!"

The Pigs began to panic, but Napoleon the 13th calmed them by announcing that he had an idea. The Pigs had considered the idea before, but had always rejected it with minimal discussion. The idea would require them to give up too many of their privileges, too much of their power, and most of their control. Napoleon the 13th told them, in quiet and calm tones, that perhaps this was the only course left open to them. To continue on the present course would ensure disaster. Either they would provoke a revolt among the animals, or, sooner or later, they would run out of animals the butcher was willing to buy.

"Okay, here is my idea," Napoleon the 13th said to the expectant assembly. "It is not a happy one, but you may like it better than what we have been doing, even though it was only in your best interest that we made these sacrifices. It pained me greatly to choose one of your number to give his or her life for the good of the community. I would cry myself to sleep each time it happened. And I prayed each night that this would be the last time, that we would climb out of our financial straits and see the light of freedom and prosperity once more."

The animals did not fully understand everything Napoleon the 13th said, but it sounded good, so they awaited the announcement of his idea.

"This suggestion has been made before, but we have always rejected it, because it meant that we would be giving up our freedom. We would be giving up complete ownership of "Animal Farm" and turning over control to our most hated enemy—Humans!"

This produced a low murmur of disapproval, but Napoleon the 13th quieted it by going on; "It appears now that the only alternative for us is to …" he paused for effect, then sighed deeply, and concluded, "…go public."

It took Napoleon the 13th and the other Pigs a while to explain what that meant. They never fully understood the economics nor the legal procedures for preparing an initial public offering. The initials "IPO" were new to them. And the thought of turning ownership over to humans, after 40 years of hard labor, sacrifice, and dedication by several generations of animals was a big cud to chew. In the end, however, they reluctantly came to the conclusion that freedom had to be sacrificed in order to obtain security, and they grudgingly agreed that once again the Pigs had advised wisely—all of them, that is, except Emerson. He was heard to mutter something about "out of the frying pan, and into the fire." No one asked him what that meant.

CHAPTER THREE

The Suits Pay a Call

The world is a dangerous place to live; not because of the people who are evil, but because of the people who don't do anything about it.

Albert Einstein

NOT MANY DAYS LATER, Napoleon the13th called another meeting to inform the animals they would soon be visited by a group of humans. "Will they be moving back onto the Farm? Into the house?" asked one of the chickens. "No," replied Squealer the 15th, speaking for Napoleon. "The humans will be here for a short visit to inspect their investment. They have no interest in living here. In fact, we will see very little of them as long as we continue to work hard and perform satisfactorily."

"What does 'perform satisfactorily' mean?" queried one of the horses, naturally interested since the horses did most of the hard work. "It means," replied the Pig in charge of communication, "that we have to make the Farm a profitable investment for the humans, or they will take their money elsewhere, and we will be back where we were a few days ago—in financial trouble—going to the butcher to bail us out."

A shudder ran through the gathering. Squealer continued, "If we make a profit for the investors, they will leave us alone, and we will all be quite content. And we will see very little of them. We will send them a pee-n-ell—uh—um—a profit-and-loss statement every three months, and once a year we will have a stockholders' meeting—which will not be held here. Instead, it will be held in some nice hotel in a nice resort, where they can de-clutter their busy minds and drink—I mean—think clearly, get to know each other better on the golf course, and make decisions and give us advice about ways in which we can make their investment more profitable. And, best of all, none of you will have to attend the meeting—just us Pigs."

"Sounds like going to a nice resort might be fun—a nice break from the routine of all the hard work we do every day," muttered another horse not so quietly. "Who's paying the bill, anyhow?"

"Well—we all do. That's one of the reasons we don't all go to the meeting. It would cost too much. Besides, only stockholders can go to the meetings, and you are not stockholders."

"Why can't we be stockholders?" one of the sheep bleated.

"You can be, if you can afford to buy stock," chuckled Squealer, and all the other Pigs laughed. "Really, you wouldn't want to go to a stockholders' meeting—beastly boring things."

"Playing golf in a fancy resort doesn't sound boring," retorted one of the chickens, who had no clue how he would ever hold a club.

"Anyway," Squealer went on, ignoring the chicken, "at noon tomorrow, the investors will be here to inspect the Farm and decide if they have invested wisely, so you must all be on your best behavior. Make sure everything is clean, and be sure to be hard at your chores as long as they are here. Don't strike up a conversation with any of them. Just smile and wave. Let us Pigs do the talking. That's what we are paid to do."

"And very well, I might add," muttered a goat in a voice so low only those closest to him heard it. A chuckle of agreement was heard by the Pigs, but they thought it best to ignore it, and went back to the farmhouse.

The Suits Pay a Call

* * *

The next morning, the Pigs were hard at work, sprucing up the yard, putting out colorful banners that said "Welcome to Animal Farm!" and "Have a nice day!" One of the Pigs was even putting a fresh coat of paint on the fence that neatly bordered the front yard. The barn and the house had been painted last month when the visit was first announced. The Farm hadn't looked this good in years. Nor had the Pigs worked so hard in years, but it was work that could not be delegated to less intelligent animals.

The animals were naturally apprehensive about the changes that were likely to take place with the new owners. Over the past 40 years, they had gradually gotten some improvements in their working conditions from the Pigs, such as small increases in their pay, but never more than just enough to pay their feed bills, which increased as well. There was never enough to allow them to put anything aside for the future. They won a 40-hour work week, with the understanding they would be paid extra for working more than 40 hours. And they even got some benefits like subsidized trips to the veterinarian if they got sick, and pay continuation while they recovered, as long as the sickness did not last too long or cost too much. They were reminded regularly that these benefits were expensive, and that it was only because the Pigs really cared about their animals that the benefits were continued at all. "After all," Napoleon the 13th was fond of repeating, "You animals are our most important asset! We could not be successful without you! We are all one big happy family!"

At noon, several long, black limousines rolled up to the farmhouse, and a couple of dozen humans—all men and all wearing blue suits, starched white shirts, and muted red ties—climbed up the steps to the front door. A few minutes later, they came out the back door, wearing hard hats, protective eye coverings, sanitary gloves, and rubber overshoes to protect them from whatever they might step in. Some even wore gauze masks to fend off offending odors. The Pigs were wearing the biggest smiles any animal had ever seen. They were busy keeping the humans out of earshot of any of the less equal animals.

The first-line supervisors—sheep dogs trained by the Pigs—were busy keeping the animals hard at their chores. Any animal caught staring at the humans was barked at. If they persisted, they would get a quick and painful nip in the nether regions.

All the animals were paid by the hour, or the piece, according to the work they did, how much they did, how well they did it, and how valuable what they did was to the Farm. They all had job descriptions that informed each one what was expected of them as part of their normal duties. Each job description had the added phrase, "…and other duties as required."— meaning that any animal could be required to do anything the first-line supervisor, or any other upperling, told them to do.

The best workers could get promoted—up to a point. A chicken, for example, could be promoted to "chief chicken," and be paid more than most other chickens, but could never be promoted to first-line supervisor. To do that, one had to graduate from obedience training—and be a dog. And we all know you can't teach a chicken to bark.

Any animal could advance his or her career through hard work, being smart and diligently learning new skills, but after a certain point, promotions came from having connections, a powerful sponsor, playing the political game correctly, or just being at the right place at the right time. And no one, no matter how smart or hardworking, could ever be promoted into the ranks of a Pig .

The tour by the dignitaries did not last long. The heat of the day, combined with the smell of the barnyard, caused most of the investors, especially the older ones, to suggest a return to the farmhouse where they could discuss "The Numbers" in air-conditioned comfort, and where they could call the office while enjoying a cool drink. When they all disappeared into the farmhouse, some of the animals began to relax a little, but the dogs reminded them that they could be watched through the windows and had better keep looking busy until the limousines left the Farm.

The discussion of "The Numbers" took a long time. What is so important about "The Numbers," the animals wondered. And what does the phrase—The Bottom Line—mean? It must be important; they keep using it, and every time someone says "The Bottom Line," there was a hush. All further discussion ceased, and quiet ruled for several minutes before a senior participant broke the silence. There must be something magical about it, maybe even religious, since the mention of the Bottom Line always produces reverential silence.

Finally, as the sun started to lower itself in the sky and the day began to cool off, The Suits climbed back into the limousines. They had surrendered the hard hats, the gloves, and the shoe protectors. They drove away in the direction from which they had come. As they drove off, the Pigs waved, smiled their exaggerated smiles, and shouted, "Come back any time!"

As soon as the last limousine was out of sight, the smiles turned into frowns of worry. Agitated conversation began amongst the Pigs. They scurried back into the farmhouse and talked to each other in loud and angry tones for over an hour. Then, suddenly, the Pigs, led by Napoleon the 13th, came out the back door and headed to where the animals were assembled, having been brought together by the dogs.

"We just want you to know that the meeting went very well. You did your work exactly as you were told to do, and they were impressed by your diligence. It is 'business as usual,' my good friends, so let's keep up the good work! There may be a few changes coming up, but they will all be very small changes, and you will be informed about them when the time is right. You have nothing to worry about. No one will be personally affected by any of the changes. We'll have another meeting in a few days, so go back to your stall, get a good night's rest, and be ready for a good, productive day tomorrow. Always remember—we are deeply grateful to each of you for the hard work you do each day. The Farm would not be successful if it weren't for all your hard work. Our job, as Pigs, is to help you be successful, because if you are successful, we are ALL successful! The Farm is successful! Long live Animal Farm!!"

And with that, all the Pigs walked single file back into the farmhouse, without a word and without looking back.

The sun went down and the dark, moonless night created a sense of eerie calm that caused the animals to retreat deep into their own thoughts. There was no conversation. None was necessary. All knew intuitively that something was astir, and it would not be in their best interest. No one had the courage to break the silence, to say aloud what all were thinking. There will be changes, and we won't like them, they thought. Do the Pigs think we are completely blind to the fear in their eyes that their smiles could not conceal? When will they learn not to under-estimate the intelligence of the animals that work for them? Emerson let out a low moan, that made sleep difficult for the animals who heard it.

CHAPTER FOUR

The Squeeze

I always expect the worst to happen, and what happens is always worse than I expected.

Henry Adams

The problem with business is management.

W. Edwards Deming

The promised meeting never took place. Instead, a memo from Napoleon the 13th to "All My Fellow Workers" informed them that the Farm was no longer called "Animal Farm."

From this day forward, we will be working for a publicly held corporation known as "Animal Firm." It will be listed on the stock exchange as "Analfir" Our opening price was 9½, but due to technical corrections and profit takers, it was at 3¼ by market closing time. This would be a good time to buy, because the price is sure to climb tomorrow. If you are interested in this "cash only" opportunity, see your supervising sheep dog and ask for the forms for purchasing stock.

Very few of the animals had ever seen cash, and no one knew for sure what 3¼ meant. One chicken has been able to save up nearly $4 in quarters once, but they discovered she had been selling half her feed to a chicken from another farm, and had nearly starved herself to death. They had to use her savings to pay the vet bills.

From that day forward, all communication from the Pigs to the other animals came as memos, office gossip, or by "trickle down," the quality of which depended upon how conscientious or how competent the "trick-lers" were in passing on useful information. If a senior vice president Pig, for example, knew a piece of information and passed it on in roughly the same form in which it was received, the recipients could consider themselves very fortunate. This did not happen very often, because, after all, information is power, and you don't retain power for long if you give it away constantly. Withholding information is an effective way to maintain control of your operation. The only difficulty is, the animals quickly checked with each other and compared messages, which made them cynical, embittered, and motivated to withhold energy and commitment.

The animals had other ways to obtain information, one of the best of which was going through the executive wastebaskets. The Pigs finally invested in a shredder, but they didn't use it all the time—certainly not as often as they should have. They would say to themselves, "Why should I go all the way down the hall to the shredder for this insignificant piece of information? It won't make any sense to them anyhow." And the memo would be rolled into a ball and sent to the wastebasket like a hoop shot. No Pig would ever retrieve an errant shot. "That's what we have janitors for." So the ducks, who most often got the janitor jobs because they were built low to the ground, would be careful to gather all the rolled up memos and deliver them to the goats, who were best at deciphering and interpreting the arcane messages contained therein. There was something in it for the goats—they could choose which memos to eat.

The most efficient and destructive form of information generation was the rumor mill. When information is lacking, it gets invented. "Wouldn't it be interesting if …." becomes, "Guess what I just heard from . . . " The reliability of a story is likely to be checked out inversely as to how interesting or how farfetched it is. All animals have an overpowering urge to be the first bearer of a tale, even two-legged ones, and a rumor can make its way around the Farm (sorry—Firm) more quickly than an email, assuming that anyone besides an executive Pig had access to a keyboard or knew how to use one.

A few days later, an "action item" came down, this time in the form of a memo carried by an executive Pig and handed to a supervising sheep dog, indicating its importance. The dog read the memo to the assembled workers as the Pig watched approvingly. The memo read:

> Effective immediately, all workers will be referred to as "associates"—a designation intended to infer dignity and enhance self-esteem among all animals in the Firm. We will no longer refer to Firm-ers as animals, workers, employees, etc. Everyone will be referred to as "associates," including executive associates.
>
> Also effective immediately, we will be implementing a cost savings program. All associates are encouraged to find ways to save money by wasting less, conserving on supplies, and ordering materials only after receiving approval from the head purchasing Pig.
>
> We have installed a suggestion box next to the back door of the Firmhouse. Suggestion forms will be available from HR. Each month, there will be a prize for the best suggestion for saving money. We need your suggestions! We welcome your ideas! Join the bandwagon and help YOUR company save money!

The Pigs seemed to be in meetings continually—one meeting after another. They complained about all the meetings they had to attend, but no one ever saw one of the Pigs outside doing any manual labor—unless the Board was having a meeting, which they did less frequently at the Firm. After the Pigs came out of a meeting, the associates would stir uneasily, wondering if there would be any announcements or memos. If a Pig was asked directly, there would be two possible responses: (1) the truth—rarely given, and rarely recognized as such if it was the truth; (2) an official white lie, because in the best judgment of the executive associates, they did not "have a need to know" the truth, or it would be too hard to explain to the ordinary mind.

There were two kinds of white lies. The first kind of white lie is one in which the Pig (it's a lot easier to say "Pig" than "executive associate") knew the answer but was not at liberty to divulge the information. In this case, some made-up but plausible story was told in place of the truth. In the second kind, the Pig did not know the answer but did not want to appear to be outside the inner circle, so the response was, "I am not at liberty to divulge that information. You will find out in due time."

Every associate had a performance review once a year, on his or her birthday, which, coincidently, was the same day as their anniversary, since each animal became part of the Firm on the day they were born. When the Firm was the Farm, animals were reviewed based on their production, and would get some kind of token increase in their feed allowance based on improvement over the previous year. When the Firm took over, the increases vanished. The average or below average associate was told there would no increase because the animal's—oops—associate's performance did not measure up to standard or the goals set at the beginning of the review period. Those associates who had excelled were told that there just wasn't enough money to give them an increase, but, in its place, each would receive a Certificate of Achievement at the next all-associates meeting—date to be announced later.

Another week went by before the next announcement came down. This time, the memo was handed to the sheep dogs by Squealer himself, who was carrying a large file folder of important-looking papers. The paper looked important because the print was very small and the size of the paper was different. It was larger, about three inches longer than the regular memo-size sheets, probably so each sheet could hold more words. Was this a cost saving measure, the associates wondered? They never had a chance to ask the question, because a great gust of wind blew the papers from Squealer's grasp. He shrieked, "Help me get those papers back!" The associates instantly went into action and were able to retrieve most of the papers, but not all.

Squealer handed each sheep dog a copy of a memo, then scurried back to the Firmhouse. He did not wait around for the memo to be read. The sheep dogs quickly surmised why; the announcement was not a happy one.

The cost savings we have all been working for have not been as great as we had hoped. We all need to make even greater sacrifices for the good of the Firm, and of all of us. We have been thinking of all the ways we could save more money, and several ideas have been considered.

We have decided that the following cost saving steps will be implemented effective immediately:

- The soft drink and candy bar machines will no longer be subsidized. You have to pay full price for your sugar treats.
- Overtime pay is no longer authorized. If you don't get your work done in eight hours a day or less, you will have to ask your sheep dog, who can get authorization for overtime pay from no one but Napoleon the 13th himself.

- Up till now, the Firm has paid 50% of the fees for your medical insurance. From now on, the Firm will pay only 20%. You will have to make up the difference, or take a cut in health coverage.
- Short-term disability coverage has been reduced from 30 days to 10 days. There will be no more long-term disability coverage.

We regret these cutbacks, but there is no other way we can meet the goals that have been set for us by the owners of the Firm. If we still cannot meet our goals, sterner steps will follow.

But we have confidence in you! We know you have what it takes to tighten your belts and work harder so we can all enjoy the success we deserve! We thank you for all your hard work and your loyalty. You are the Firm's most important asset!

"Look at this!" screamed one of the goats, just as the sheep dogs finished reading the memo. "This is one of the papers that Squealer dropped! I was getting ready to eat it when something caught my eye. I don't understand it all, but it seems . . . it seems . . ."

One of the older goats grabbed the sheet of paper and began to read it aloud. It was entitled, Executive Compensation Program. The old goat read it over quickly, then said: "It appears that the owners of the Firm have come up with an interesting way to encourage the Pigs to keep costs low. The lower the operating costs, the bigger their bonuses."

"That means they are increasing their bonuses by keeping our pay increases low and by taking away our benefits," muttered the wise old bull, Emerson, in the loudest voice anyone had heard him use.

"That's what it looks like to me," replied the goat. Angry muttering and occasional expletives peppered the air.

"Let's organize! We'll form a union!"

"Should have thought of that years ago. It's too late now. They'll just fire us all."

"Where would we go? Has anyone heard of any farms looking for more animals?"

"Let's take over the house and run the Pigs off, just like our ancestors ran Jones out."

"What would that accomplish? The owners would just hire more Pigs. And they wouldn't come after us with guns this time—they'd come after us with lawyers!"

"Oh, my God!" cried the animals, almost in chorus, almost in harmony.

The mention of lawyers pretty well brought the free-for-all discussion to an end, and the animals just looked at each other sadly.

"Okay," said one of the older horses. "If they are going to cut our pay and benefits, we can just work less hard. We will work just hard enough to keep from getting sent to the butcher, but not nearly as hard as we could work if we were being treated fairly."

So the animals agreed to try hard to look busy enough in order not to attract the attention of the Pigs or the sheep dogs, but to cut way back on what they were really capable of doing. They also agreed to review their job descriptions and to refuse to do anything not clearly spelled out in the document.

"It might be hard to just outright refuse, but we can at least work even more slowly or pretend we don't know how to do the work, or make so many mistakes they'll wish they hadn't asked us to do it in the first place."

"Right! They'll have to spend so much time supervising us they won't be able to do their own work! Re-work is expensive!"

The animals all agreed the new "work ethic" would begin the next day. Emerson just smiled, keeping his head low so it would not be seen by any but those closest to him.

CHAPTER FIVE

The Motivational Speaker

> I have discovered the secret of happiness. I don't go to meetings. If we all stopped going to meetings, we could get our work done and go home by 1 o'clock.
>
> Art Buchwald

A year went by. The first annual meeting of the Board and stockholders (pretty much one and the same) of Animal Firm had taken place in Bermuda. The leading Pigs—Napoleon the 13th, Squealer and a handful of others, returned, reeking of suntan lotion, wearing souvenir T-shirts, expensive resort sunglasses, and smoking Cuban cigars. They complained about how much work they had to do, but could not quite conceal the grins of self-satisfaction as they saw the looks of envy from the younger Pigs.

The animals hoped for a meeting telling them all the decisions affecting them, but all they got was a memo:

> To all associates of Animal Firm: this is to inform you that everything went very well at the annual meeting in Bermuda. The Board and stockholders are satisfied with the work you have done in the last year. Bonus checks for those

of you who are bonus-eligible will be in your mail boxes within the next three working days.

Goals for the coming fiscal year have been set. We are committed to improving our profitability by 10% and to maintain current spending levels. No increases in expenditures for supplies are authorized without my personal review and signature, and no capital expenditures of any kind will be approved by anyone but myself.

As a reward for your hard work last year, we have a special treat for you. In two weeks, we will have a special guest for a day, a world famous motivational speaker. His name is "Ace" Azel, and they call him "Ambassador to the Animal World." I have heard him speak, and he is one of the most inspiring speakers I have ever heard! I know you will find him as exciting and as motivational as I did.

"Ace" will tell us how to get more done by having a positive mental attitude. There are no limits to what we can do if we put our minds to it! He will tell us how.

Bringing "Ace" to the Firm is an expression of the high regard I have for each of you associates, and how much I personally appreciate all that you have done to make the Firm successful. You are our most important asset! It will cost a lot of money to bring "Ace" here, so please give him all your attention and show him every courtesy.

I am, as always, at your service.

Napoleon the 13th, CEO and President

"What's a bonus?" asked one of the chickens. "And what is 'bonus-eligible?'" a duck chimed in. "What is a mail box?" asked a young lamb? No animal had a ready answer. Emerson exhaled loudly, toed the turf in front of him, and told them in his deep, rumbling voice so rarely heard any more;

"A bonus is a cash reward for doing a good job, in the opinion of those who pass out the bonuses. And, if you don't have a mail box, you most likely are not eligible to receive a bonus."

The animals looked at one another. Not one of them had a mailbox, not even Emerson, who had sired hundreds of prize-winning offspring over the years. He knew his siring days were over. Many of the other animals knew it as well, but they were quiet about it. They knew that, as soon as the Pigs found out that Emerson was eating good food but not making little beefers, he would be on his way to the Great Bullpen in the Sky.

Twelve days later, a long, black stretch limo pulled up in front of the Firmhouse, The door was opened by a spiffy supernumerary, and out leapt a donkey, wearing what must have been a very expensive gray suit, nattily tailored, with a dazzlingly loud silk necktie, a fresh boutonniere in his lapel and a carefully folded handkerchief in his jacket pocket. The donkey strutted toward the front door flashing a great, toothy smile, while one of his lackeys checked him over for loose threads, lint, or dandruff. The donkey skipped every other stair as he charged toward the front door, which was being held open for him by Squealer.

The celebrity was met with a lot of loud and joyful greetings, back-slapping, and laughter. The noise emanating from the Firmhouse got the attention of the barnyard associates, so they gathered in the shadow of the Founding Quadrapeds to observe whatever proceedings were about to be unveiled. They didn't have to wait long. The donkey charged out the back door toward the barnyard, teeth glistering behind widely parted lips, followed by an entourage of acolytes. Lastly trotted Napoleon the 13th, regally bringing up the rear. He quickly moved to the front, where he introduced the well-appointed donkey to the assembled associates.

"Friends and associates of Animal Firm, it gives me great pleasure to present to you today for your listening and learning pleasure an animal who needs no introduction—one who has traveled the world, been attended to by kings, queens and presidents, has spoken to crowds in excess of one hundred thousand in crowded sports arenas, has had an audience with the Pope, the Metropolitan, the Archbishop of Canterbury, and Pat Robertson. We are unusually fortunate to have one of this stature and world-renown visit our humble firm and speak to us. Without further ado, I give you . . . Ace Azel!!"

When the roar of the crowd subsided, 'Ace' strode to the makeshift platform that bore a small microphone, straightened his tie, flashed his biggest smile, and began to elocute on the virtues and power of having a positive mental attitude. The animals were quickly in his thrall. His command of the language, his grippingly told tales of pathos and perseverance, his mastery of the emotional heart strings, had everyone present alternately laughing and weeping. Had he called for it, the animals would have crowned him king on the spot. He led them in chants and cheers, songs and prayers, and they followed along happily, enthusiastically, begging for more. Before his speech was half finished, each and every animal present was convinced nothing would stop him or her from achieving whatever goals they set their newly positive minds to accomplish. By the end of his talk, the animals felt like gods.

As he turned to leave, 'Ace' reminded them that there was a table in the back with books, tapes, autographed pictures, pencils, pens, ribbons, buttons, bumper stickers, T-shirts, caps, illustrated "red letter edition" Bibles complete with maps of the Holy Land and a picture of Ace in the front, mugs, toothbrushes, post cards, and schedules of upcoming events. Your credit card happily accepted.

And he was gone.

As soon as he left, the animals felt emotionally drained, exhausted and a little bit downcast. A form of postpartum depression began to settle over them as they trudged back to their stalls, pens and coops. None of them could afford any of the souvenirs, and of course, there was no tape player to play an audiocassette had anyone the wherewithal to acquire one. And who ever heard of a credit card? "Mail boxes, my ass," one of the mules quipped unintentionally.

The next morning, their spirits were brightened by the sound of 'Ace' Azel's voice coming over the Firm's boom box. Napoleon the 13th, in a fit of generosity, had purchased a set of tapes to be played for the animals each morning as they were waking up to motivate them to get to work—faster, harder, longer! "That's how we will make the Firm even more profitable in the coming 12 months. And if you liked 'Ace,' wait till next year!"

Emerson rolled his eyes at the promise of more such entertainment. Very few saw it, but those who did took note. The word quickly spread around the barnyard that Emerson was not buying this pitch.

CHAPTER SIX

The Day of the Chicken

Democracy means simply the bludgeoning of the people,
by the people, for the people.

Oscar Wilde

In the middle of the firmyard, about 100 yards from the Firmhouse, stood a large chicken coop, surrounded by a ten foot tall chicken wire fence. It was intentionally placed at a distance from the dwelling place of the Pigs because Pigs cannot stand the smell of chickens or the sound of their incessant cackling.

Inside the coop were all kinds of chickens: black, white, red, speckled, layers and fryers, roosters, hens and chicks—a disorderly house if ever there was such. The Pigs were not scientific farmers, and didn't know one breed from another. They collected the eggs and sold them, and occasionally they sold a fryer to a local buyer. The Pigs never ate eggs. Eggs are generally eaten with bacon or sausage, the very thought of which gave the Pigs goose bumps. They didn't want to think about that.

Early one morning, there was a ruckus in the chicken coop. One of the older, more self-important hens was busy exercising her superiority at the expense of a young chick who had somehow stepped out of line. Bertha, the old hen, was convinced that Heather, the young chick, was getting too cocky for her age. Furthermore, she was of egg-producing age, but had chosen to postpone motherhood in order to acquire more useful skills, such as learning to fly.

Heather ate all the chicken feed she could get her beak into, but shunned the daily delivery of garbage coming from the Firmhouse kitchen. "She's an uppity chick—doesn't know her place in the pecking order," clucked Bertha.

Chickens are not very bright animals, and they tend to overreact to every stimulus. They will follow the rare assertive bird with no questions asked. Bertha learned to be assertive at an early age, so she had pretty much managed the chicken yard most of her adult life. Not many of the chickens did her bidding with enthusiasm, but chickens are not trouble-makers or rebels. Most of them, most of the time, just did what they were told, and Bertha liked to tell them what to do. All of them, that is, except Heather.

Heather was ambitious, and smarter than your average chick. She was an Episcopalian, and Bertha was a Southern Baptist. Bertha was a Republic-hen and Heather was a Demo-cackle. Heather was capable of flying around the chicken yard, and Bertha hated her for that. Bertha called her nasty names and made foul references to the end product of Heather's digestive process, in return for which Heather would swoop and dive at Bertha like a fighter pilot.

The day finally came when Heather found herself flying higher than the chicken wire fence. As the other chickens gasped and clucked, Heather flew the coop!

This came to the attention of the Pigs, who decided they could not afford to lose the younger generation of chickens who worshipped Heather and might follow her example. There already was a club of young chickens practicing their flying skills. They called themselves "Birds of a Heather," became vegetarians, refused to eat garbage, exercised daily, and practiced yoga. Bertha was interrogated, and the Pigs asked her to produce a white paper. She wrote that the moral tone of the chicken house had deteriorated because of Heather's influence. The young chickens were leaving the one true church and were joining more liberal denominations, New Age groups, and some, she speckled, were secretly practicing birth control, as evidenced by their low egg production. She concluded, "We must pass laws against the things they enjoy doing!"

The Pigs concluded the chickens must have their wings clipped. Not having opposable thumbs, the Pigs outsourced the clipping chore to a few of the boys from the village who were always looking for a few extra coins. They didn't much like what the Pigs offered them—calling it "chicken feed" and referred to the Pigs as "chicken poop," but they took the work.

The first clipping day was a long one, since the chickens were the most numerous of the Firm animals. They were very productive of good cash crops—eggs, chicken meat, and feathers—and they were cheap to feed, since most of them were willing to eat table scraps as well as chicken feed. As the first clipping took all day, several of the boys quit. The work was hard, undigni-fied, and the chickens were not always cooperative. Turnover was high and the supply of new boys was limited. But if their wages were increased, it would have a negative affect on the Firm's pee-n-ell, and thus the Pigs' bonuses. Turn-over was costly, it took time to train a new chicken wing clipper, but the cost of turnover does not appear on the pee-n-ell, so the bonuses were not affected.

One of the boys, who was more clever than most, figured out that it was not necessary to clip both wings on every chicken. If only one wing was clipped, flying would be very difficult. A one-winged chicken could only fly in circles. If only one wing needed to be clipped, the Pigs could let half the boys go and raise the pay of the ones who remained, thus reducing turno-ver without increasing the costs to the Pigs. The clever boy, Kernel Sanders, delighted the Pigs with his proposal, and told him to organize it. His com-pany became a spin-off of the Firm and was incorporated as a subchapter S corporation called "Chick Flickers, LLC."

The chickens came to like the new arrangement. They got into the habit of returning to the same clipper each time, formed friendships, shared secrets, sought advice, and told chicken jokes.

Some of the boys were left-handed, and they found it easiest to clip a chicken's left wing. The other chickens had their right wings clipped. The left wing chickens could only fly in clockwise circles. The others, who flew in counter-clockwise circles, thought the left wing birds strange, and they avoided them, choosing to hang out with their own kind. Each claimed to be doing it the correct and proper way and ridiculed the others who not only wouldn't, but couldn't, straighten up and fly right.

The friendly rivalry turned bitter over time. Bertha became the leader and clucksperson for the right wing chickens, and one of Heather's followers, Allouette (a name she chose for herself), led the left wingers. They adopted slogans, made banners, and held cockusses to assemble their views into campaign platforms. They made big issues out of concerns the other animals thought inconsequential. The chickens saw themselves as the hard core of their respective parties, and regarded the rest of the animals as the swing vote.

Not all the Pigs were interested in the proceedings, but a few thought important things were happening and wanted to be able to influence the outcome. These Pigs donated bags of chicken feed to their favorite party. They came to be called "Fat Pigs."

The Republic-hens were opposed to egg control, strongly supported the maintenance of good relations with the Pigs, in spite of the obvious ethical lapses, in order to continue the steady flow of chicken feed. They also called for loopholes in the chicken feed allowance as a reward for superior egg production.

Under no circumstance should a chicken be required to share his or her chicken feed with a less fortunate chicken.

The Demo-cackles advocated freedom of choice in the matter of egg production, called for the development of new technologies to make the chickens less dependent on cheap, imported chicken feed, and insisted that the big egg producers assume their social responsibility and share their largesse with the less fortunate chickens.

Bertha held a news conference. All the media dogs were invited to attend, and they all showed up with an impressive array of equipment for recording the event. Bertha announced the forthcoming election.

"The time has come for a showdown! Now is the time for all Firm animals to stand up for what they believe in! The left wing chickens want to take from us hardworking Republic-hens the chicken feed we so richly deserve and use it to fatten up the scrawny birds that don't produce as many eggs as we do!"

"We believe that we should be allowed to keep all the chicken feed that we have earned by the sweat of our coxcombs! We demand lower taxes on our chicken feed! We call upon our leaders to support the suppliers of cheap imported chicken feed! And stop feeding those chickens who practice egg control!!"

There was a loud squawk of approval from the right wing chickens and half of the swing vote. The media dogs stooped over their writing pads and videocams. Then, suddenly there was a stir at the edge of the assembled animals. There, striding toward the microphones, was Heather!

"I want to make a statement!" Bertha was stunned into silence. The left wing chickens squawked their noisy approval.

"I left this community because I was not allowed the freedom to express my views, live my values, and practice my unorthodox lifestyle. Now we have come to a crossroads, and the future of our community is at stake. I have decided to return—in response to a loud and clear call from my fellow patriots—to lead a campaign to win back for the common animals a chance to live in dignity and self-respect!"

A long and loud squawk of approval from the left wing chickens was supported by the other half of the swing vote. It was hard to tell by the voices which side was ahead, so the campaign began with the undecided voters serving as the target of all the rhetoric of the next several weeks. The media dogs took frequent polls, which showed consistently a 50/50 split—with the allowance of a 5% margin of error. The Republic-hens had most of the chicken feed, donated by the Fat Pigs, but the left wing chickens were more numerous. If they would only turn up at the polls on election day and vote for the party's choice, and not scatter their votes among a bunch of splinter candidates! The sheep had a favorite son, the cows couldn't support any chicken candidate, and the horses announced they were going to boycott the election. None of the ducks even bothered to register. What was in it for them? They didn't eat chicken feed!

A few days before the election, the Firm was shocked by a tragedy that threw the entire population into a state of frenzy. The politicians were hysterically trying to pin the blame on their opponents. Dozens of corpses of dead chickens littered the chicken yard. Investigations were called for, explanations demanded. "Who?" "Why?" "How?" "Someone must be hung!" The media dogs were forced to sit under hot lights and talk incessantly, trying to stretch five minutes of information into hours of programming without too much obvious repetition. The commercials gave them small breaks to figure out how to say the same things in different ways. And the commercials were inevitably in very bad taste.

What had happened? Late at night, enemy agents from a foreign country snuck into the chicken coop and senselessly murdered dozens of helpless, unarmed chickens, all civilians and noncombatants—young, old, male, female. Heather had escaped by flying overhead, and Bertha survived by hiding behind her supporters, many of whom were injured. The sight the next morning was revolting. Hardened law enforcement officials wept openly. Cynical media dogs vomited. The surviving chickens were delirious, and could not give coherent witness reports. Nurse Scratchet tried sedating some of the chickens to calm them down enough to be able to talk, but it still took hours for the details to leak out.

What finally emerged, after half a day of gathering scraps of evidence and bits of testimony, was that enemy agents from the nearby dark forest, probably a sly fox and a perfidious raccoon, had gotten through the chicken wire fence and had gone on a rampage of wanton killing.

How did they get through the entire Firm, then through the chicken wire fence, without being detected? They must have had help from the inside. Certainly there was malfeasance and incompetence in the security system. The Pigs had installed a "fool proof" system to protect the animals from critters and varmints from the deep, dark forest. Only the Pigs knew how to turn the system off. Only the Pigs could open the gate in the chicken wire fence. They had an apparent motive—a desire to botch the election, which might take away some of their power.

"Our system of public peace has been forever besmirched!" the Republic-hens cried hysterically. "Someone must pay the price for this travesty, this incredible incompetence, this . . . treason! We must suspend civil liberties until the crisis is firmly behind us and we can return to a system based on law and order!"

"We must hire more police dogs!" squawked the Demo-cackles. "Even if it means raising taxes!"

The campaign had lost some of its momentum in a few days. People got tired of hearing the same old, unexciting speeches and were not interested in watching the debates. A couple of the candidates got more than their share of bad publicity when someone discovered that one of them had tried smoking chicken feed when he was a teenager and the other had a secret liaison with a young chick who bore him a love-egg years ago. Other than that, people stopped watching the multimillion dollar infomercials and became outright angry when their favorite sitcom or football game was pre-empted to allow yet another political speech to air in its place. Now, with this cataclysmic event to talk about, victim compensation plans were promised, and assurances that, if elected, corrective measures would be installed to ensure that such a tragedy would never be repeated.

The Pigs, especially the Fat Pigs, were maintaining a discrete silence and distance from the proceedings. Media dogs were busy polling the voters every 24 hours, coming up with conflicting results and drawing dubious conclusions. Election Day approached with no clear mandate from the voters. Some of the animals called for war on the critters and varmints in the deep, dark forest, with the special intent of bringing the sly fox and the perfidious raccoon to justice. The right wing chickens were the most adamant about going to war. The left wing chickens held marches and demonstrations, calling for peace and diplomatic solutions to the problems of the deep, dark forest.

Election Day came and went. The Republic-hens won by the slimmest of margins, and the Demo-cackles demanded recounts and investigations of election fraud. Many changes were promised, but not much happened. Things went on pretty much as they did before the election. The lot of the chickens did not improve, which gave the left wing chickens all the fodder they needed to get started on the next election campaign. Heather flew the coop again, went on a speaking tour and wrote a book. Bertha, the presiding chicken, had to take all the chicken poop the Demo-cackles could throw at her. No one ever caught the sly fox or the perfidious raccoon.

CHAPTER SEVEN

Left versus Right

It isn't that they can't see the solution—they can't see the problem.

G. K. Chesterton

Education is an admirable thing, but it is well to remember from time to time that nothing that is worth knowing can be taught.

Oscar Wilde

When the hubbub died down, many of the animals not of the poultry persuasion wondered what the difference was between Republic-hens and Demo-cackles, between left wing and right wing. A few of them asked Emerson, the wise old bull, to explain. He agreed, and a couple of days later, a large group of animals of all sorts and sizes gathered in the barn, where Emerson had set up a chart pad with a supply of colored markers.

"Be patient with me," Emerson began. "It is not easy to draw on these chart pads without an opposable thumb." With a colored marker clenched in his teeth, he drew the following diagram:

"This is a graphic rendition of the political spectrum. What that means is that most of us fall somewhere along this line, depending on what our political preferences are and how strongly we hold those preferences. For instance, if you are a Demo-cackle and are unlikely to support any candidate who is not a Demo-cackle, you would be part of the 20% on the left, called the Demo-cackle base. If you are a Demo-cackle but on occasion you can be persuaded to vote for someone other than a Demo-cackle, you would be in the 20% of the Demo-cackle spectrum who are called moderates.

"The same designations apply to those on the Republic-hen end of the spectrum. Those in the middle are called Independ-hens and can go either way, depending on who they find most persuasive. And you can see that no one wins an election without persuading a large number of Independ-hens to vote for him or her.

"There is a problem with describing political preferences using a flat spectrum like this—it is way too simplified. Let me try to draw another diagram to give you what I consider to be a more realistic and accurate explanation of how we decide to cast our ballots. Bear with me—this is much more complex than my first drawing:

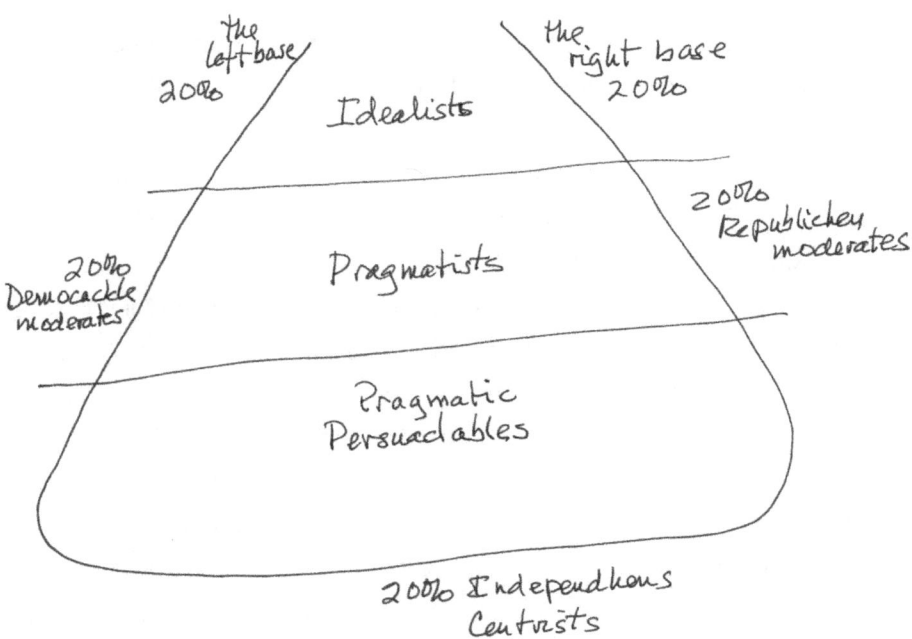

"As you can see, the flat spectrum is more accurately shaped like a horse shoe, with the left end and the right end fairly close together. There is a reason for this. Both the left and right bases—about 20% of the voters in each category—are composed of people we call "idealists." That means they see things in binary terms; they are either good or bad, black or white, either/or. You are for us or you are against us. There is no middle ground, no compromising. They see the world as it could be, as they would like it to be—if this was a perfect world.

"The moderates of both parties and the Independ-hens are called pragmatists. That is, they admit we do not live in a perfect world, that we cannot hold out to the death for our ideals, and we may have to come up with some messy compromises from time to time in order to move on. You would think they would always win every election because they comprise 60% of the voters, but they are easily persuaded by skilled rhetoric, misleading advertising, and the condition of their wallets. Idealists don't have to ask the "what if" questions because their minds are already made up early in the contest. Pragmatists often will hem and haw until they step into the voting booth.

"How does someone become an idealist? How does one become a prag-matist? I think it has to do with hardwiring of the brain. We are born with a predisposition to be one or the other. There has been a good bit of research to suggest that a left wing idealist who becomes disenchanted for whatever reason with his or her identification with the left wing of their party is more likely to go to the right wing idealist side than to the pragmatist side. And the reverse is true of a disenchanted partisan on the right. This is because, temperamentally, they are more comfortable as an inflexible idealist of either stripe than they would be as an uncertain person sloshing around in the pragmatic middle. They require certainty, and will quickly, automati-cally, move toward that place of certainty. Pragmatists can tolerate ambigu-ity more easily than idealists can.

"Unfortunately, in recent years we have had to make our peace with the idea that most of our decisions and actions, including political ones, are based on emotion rather than reason. When reason and emotion clash, the latter almost always wins. When a farm or a firm survives over the long haul, it is more likely to be the result of luck than of wise leadership."

The barn was silent for several minutes. Finally, said the largest and oldest goat, "I'm glad I don't have a goat vote. For me, it's all too remote."

CHAPTER EIGHT

The Consultants Arrive

We are often wrong, but we are never uncertain.
Ancient consultant aphorism

The wicked are wicked no doubt, and they go astray and they fall and they come by their deserts; but who can tell the mischief which the very virtuous do?
William Makepeace Thackeray

During the 1980s, the Human world was being barraged by a spate of books of two types. The first type, most popular, usually read and frequently put into practice for a short while, were diet and self-help books. Second were books about management. The message of these books was to purvey the latest management fad of the season. Their theme, generally, was that, if managers treated people right—that is, with dignity and respect—they in turn would do the company right by giving exceptional customer service.

A prolonged study of the reading habits of business executives proved that they rarely read books. This study was conducted informally by observing what was being read in the first class section of most airlines—business newspapers, reports, magazines—but almost never books, except for an occasional fast-paced novel. If an executive was given a business book and urged to read it, he or she usually gave it to a subordinate with instructions to summarize it into one page of bullets. If an executive was particularly taken by a topic or an author, he or she might purchase an audiocassette summary and listen to it while commuting. But, to sit and read a business book, taking notes, and using a highlighter, rarely happened.

Therefore, the business books that flooded the market after 1980 did little more to the workplace than change the vocabulary by introducing words and phrases like "excellence," "alignment," "empowerment," "mission statement," "vision and values," "corporate culture," "the power of goal-setting," "total quality," "reengineering," "the human factor," "the fifth discipline," "organizational transformation," and finally, "servant leadership."

A few of these books, written by consultants with good ideas they thought businessmen ought to try, did manage to make it to Animal Firm. The Pigs, being executive associates, did not read them, but they propped them up on the shelf so they looked impressive. Emerson the bull heard about these books from the ducks, which in their janitorial work had to move them from one dusty spot to another. They reported the titles and subtitles to Emerson who conspired with them to bring him one book at a time. He read them and returned them via the ducks before they were missed. In the process, Emerson learned what humans in management were talking about—a workplace that revolved around teamwork and collaboration, effective two-way communication rooted in honesty and trust; "resource providers" instead of bosses, "implementers" instead of hourly workers—the replacement of hierarchical command-and-control structures with floating project teams, matrix organizations—motivation by the mission of the organization instead of money, and a desire to please the customer instead of the fear of the boss.

Emerson pondered these concepts, wondering if they had any applicability to animals—these animals in particular. Emerson was jaded, but not cynical. For a bull, he was remarkably optimistic and hopeful. He thought even the Pigs could change. He was wise enough to know, however, that no one can change another—that true change comes from inside only—that coercion brings at best only temporary change, and then only as long as there is a foolproof and constant enforcement system.

Somehow, the Pigs must be given evidence that using some of these new management ideas would be in the best interest of Animal Firm, and ultimately in the best interest of the Pigs themselves. Emerson knew he could provide the leadership and the other animals would follow him until a younger, more energetic animal took his place. Is permanent change possible? That issue troubled him, and no amount of reading of books on change processes that work, that bring about lasting change, relieved him of his uncertainties.

* * *

One fine March day, the animals noticed a flurry of activity around the Firmhouse. The Pigs were unusually busy about something, and the ducks had found nothing in the wastebaskets to tip them off. About midmorning, two impressive autos drove up, and several suits and briefcases appeared, attached to Humans. The conversation inside lasted for hours. When the cars finally left in the late afternoon, the animals hoped there would be some news about the meeting, but no news was forthcoming.

Two days later, the same drill—lots of activity around the house, two cars with well-dressed humans pulling up front two hours before lunch and staying until two hours before supper. Again, no information was to be had.

Two weeks went by before the next expensive automobile drove up the dusty road to the Firmhouse. This time, instead of Humans, a pair of well-dressed owls walked up to the front door to be greeted by the Pigs. After only a short visit, the menagerie left the house and trudged to the barnyard, where all the animals were waiting with peaked interest. And not a little anxiety.

Napoleon the 13th showed up—a rarity—and the animals realized this was not just another pep talk. He didn't say anything—Squealer did the talking—but Napoleon the 13th's presence ensured that everything that was said was to be taken with great seriousness.

Squealer cleared his throat, then pulled a piece of paper close to his glasses and began to talk. He introduced the two owls and told the animals they would be working with Animal Firm for the next few months. They are "consultants," he explained, and they will be helping us all as we go through an exciting change in the nature of our business—something called a merger.

"A merger!" snorted Emerson, who had read a good bit about mergers in the Pigs' books. "A merger with what? And to what economic advantage? What do we associates get out of it?"

Squealer was taken aback, shocked that Emerson said anything at all. He was generally silent. Squealer was stunned that he knew anything about mergers. He started to stammer an answer when Napoleon the 13th announced that the meeting was over and instructed the owls to take over and "earn your fee." The Pigs returned to the house, leaving the owls standing there looking sheepish.

Emerson glared at the owls and demanded, "Well?" The owls sprang into action, with the help of a young turtledove who recently graduated from a hotshot MBA program. She had gone unnoticed up till now. They set up a flip chart loaded with fresh newsprint, an easel for prepared charts, and an overhead slide projector and screen. They proceeded to take turns making a presentation designed to help the animals understand what a merger is and how it would affect them. The turtledove ran around manipulating the audio-visual equipment, saying nothing.

"A merger is like a marriage between two organizations," the first owl, whose name was Henry, began. "Two organizations go through a courtship called "due diligence," until an agreement is struck, the purpose of which is to combine the organizations into one organization that has improved prospects for turning a profit."

"Is the other organization a farm like us?" asked Emerson.

The other owl, named Homer, jumped in at this point: "Yes, it is a farm—of sorts. It's more like a stable. It's a farm that raises race horses."

"Race horses are very different from plow horses," Emerson sagely observed. "And I can imagine they have no chickens or ducks or sheep or other animals, just race horses."

"That's pretty close to being accurate," Henry responded, while the turtledove looked on approvingly. She had no name—yet.

Then Emerson astonished the consultants with a deluge of questions. "How will the organizations be restructured? Will there be layoffs? How will you handle the cultural adjustments? After all, we all know that race horses are arrogant prima donnas who aren't strong enough to pull a plow or a wagon. And they will probably be terrified of the chickens and ducks running around their feet. They will certainly have no use for sheep, cattle, and the kind of strong, hardworking horses we have around here. They will get all the good food and won't clean up after themselves. And they all have a crew of Humans to wash them, brush them and exercise them. They are spoiled rotten, and they will lord it over those of us who have to do hard work to get our food."

After a pause, Henry, who seemed to be the chief, said slowly and carefully, choosing his words like a chicken picking maggots out of the swill: "That's why we are here—to ease the transition between the two organizations. The differences in your corporate cultures are immense, and to throw the two companies together without careful planning, training, coaching, and guidance from outsiders who can act with detachment and objectivity. And you, Mr. Bull—I didn't get your name . . ."

"Emerson."

"Mr. Emerson, you obviously have done a bit of study on this issue. I'm going to recommend that you be put in charge of training. We will help you—provide you with the training materials and training skills—because we want you to succeed. If you are successful, we are successful!"

"Heard that one before," muttered Emerson under his breath so the consultants would not hear.

* * *

Within a few weeks, noticeable changes began to take place. Some of the strongest horses were transferred to the other location to do the hard work the race horses couldn't, or wouldn't, do. Work began on a new building on the grounds of Animal Firm. The animals were told it was a new stable, for the animals soon to be added to the inventory. And was it posh! No expense was spared on the new edifice. The animals looked at their own dingy surroundings that had not been improved upon in two decades—not even a paint job. It was hard not to be resentful. It became a lot worse when some of the new tenants began to move into their digs. What incredible arrogance! What conceit! What just plain bad manners!

Emerson was, in fact, appointed "director of training and development" and given a staff and a budget. The consultants turned him into a trainer of trainers. He was too "laid back," too "professorial," too "conceptual" to be a trainer, but he knew the concepts that needed to be communicated. He had a knack for creating good training materials and clever analogies that clarified ideas for the others. His job, then, was to train his staff—younger, more hip, more energetic than he—to turn his content into a workshop that was entertaining, highly interactive, very experiential, intended to motivate associates to change their behavior so they would be a "better fit" for the new environment.

They learned about corporate culture, especially about the difference between a "work horse" and a "race horse" culture. They learned how to create a mission statement, a vision, what the corporate values were, and how to accommodate their own mission/vision/values with those of the corporation. The objective was to reduce the impact of cultural differences so the two halves of the new conglomerate could work together effectively, united by a common commitment to the new mission, no longer divided by "old emotional baggage."

Emerson went about his duties faithfully, steadily, and with an expertise gained from much exposure to the business literature he had read over the years. The owls were amazed at what he had learned. On more than one occasion, Emerson spotted them pouring over a book he had mentioned so they could discuss it with him intelligently.

The animals, in the meantime, enjoyed the workshops because they got a day or two away from work, the trainers told great stories and jokes—even showed some good video clips—and they returned to work enthused about the possibility of making the workplace more "humane." It might have worked, if some of the supervisors—the sheepdogs—had been trained as well. That lacking, the supervisors felt threatened by the new ideas and the loss of control they might have to deal with if any of these ideas were actually implemented. So, one by one, the sheepdogs would sit down with a newly liberated animal, fresh from a training session, and have a heart-to-heart talk about "the real world" in which we have to do business in order to survive, especially with the competition from the race horses, who make us look bad when we don't keep up with them.

Six months later, the owls disappeared, never to return. Emerson was told he would have to run the training department without their help. Not long after that, Emerson was instructed to dismantle the training department—it was no longer cost-effective. He was instructed to return his staff to their former positions, unless they preferred to take a package and find employment elsewhere.

"Isn't it interesting," Emerson mused, "that when the going gets tough, the first thing to get cut is training. Kinda like—when the team is losing games, cancel practices. On the other hand, how effective can training be when workers are learning new skills, but supervisors are not? Maybe training *is* a waste of time and money." He remembered having read somewhere the words of a famous philosopher, whose name he could not remember—"I think, therefore, I am." It seems, he smirked to himself, that the philosophy of business is—"There is a bottom line, therefore, I do not have to think, feel, or have compassion."

They seem to have gotten Descartes before Horace, Emerson thought to himself, bovinely.

CHAPTER NINE

Team Building at the Firm

Blessed is he who has found his work; let him ask no other blessedness. He has a work, a life purpose; he has found it, and he will follow it....Labor is life!

Thomas Carlyle

Without work, all life goes rotten. But when work is soulless, life stifles and dies.

Albert Camus

Blessed is the man who has some congenial work, some occupation in which he can put his heart, and which affords a complete outlet to all the forces that are within him.

John Burroughs

Emerson was strolling through the field behind the barn on a cloudy, cool afternoon when he was approached by a goat named Rudy. Rudy was upset because he watched a sheep named Martha taking food from someone else's bin. He felt it was his duty to report this infraction to Emerson.

"Have you confronted Martha on this issue?" Emerson asked.

"Well—no."

"In that case, let's call Martha in here and the three of us will discuss it together."

"Oh, but I don't want to cause any problems!" (Read: I don't want to get a reputation as a tattler.)

"You've already caused a problem. Now we have to solve it."

"But . . .but. . . "

"The alternative is for you to go out there and do the honest thing and tell Martha to her face that you have a problem with what you saw and that you need her help to solve it. Then give her a chance to tell her side of the story, and listen carefully to what she has to say. If you can resolve the issue between you, very well. If not, then both of you come back to me and we'll do problem-solving together"

"I'll do that! Thanks for your help!"

There is a fifty-fifty chance that the confrontation will actually take place, depending on the courage and integrity of the erstwhile tattler. Half the time, the meeting does not occur, but 100% of time, one can be sure the tattler will consider a different course of action the next time.

Emerson had read, among other things, some good books on organizational psychology. From them he learned how to create an environment in which a spirit of teamwork, collaboration, and camaraderie could thrive. A team that works must be built on trust. He learned that the absolute death of this environment was something called "passive-aggressive behavior." Simply defined, passive-aggressive behavior is operating with a hidden agenda—one designed to further one's own goals at the expense of community goals.

Passive-aggressive behavior can be managed, but it takes courage and insight on the part of the leader as well as the followers. For example, one form of passive-aggressive behavior is tattling. A community member feels wronged by another, but rather than confronting the other and trying positively to work out a solution to the problem, the member takes the problem to the leader for solution. This is called "delegating upward." The adept leader quickly recognizes this brand of passive-aggressive behavior and nips it in the bud.

Whenever a group of creatures, Human or otherwise, are brought together in one place, there is a natural drive to establish and protect your place in the pecking order, to know where one stands relative to the others, to be able to look down on some while avoiding the error of failing to defer appropriately to others. It's been called "the smarts to know when to kick butt and when to kiss butt."

Animal Firm was such an organization, with a clearly but wordlessly understood hierarchy. The Pigs began the process when they announced that, while all animals are equal, some are more equal than others. Within the barnyard, animals were valued by such qualities as physical strength, ability to learn useful skills, and the talent for producing economically valuable products. Horses were strong—not very smart—but their strength was essential for the success of the Firm, so their cerebral insufficiency was overlooked. Dogs were able to learn tricks that entertained the others and to please their masters by running errands and demonstrating unconditional loyalty and affection. Bulls were valued for producing cows. Cows were valued for producing milk. Chickens produced eggs, sheep made wool, and so forth. Pigeons were lowest on the totem pole. All they could produce was pigeon poop. The other animals referred to pigeons as "flying rats."

All things considered, the animal community at Animal Firm was pretty solid. The barnyard animals were knitted together by a common enemy— the Pigs. The Pigs found common cause with the barnyard animals by their joint antipathy toward Humans. The authority of Napoleon the 13th kept the animals in line and prevented the Pigs from overstepping their appropriate bounds in indelicate manifestations of *hubris*. As the unquestioned descendant of the Founder, he was the only animal that humans were willing to talk to when decisions were to be made.

The animals always had a leader—Emerson at present, whose authority was rooted in inarguable qualities such as wisdom, learning, exemplary listening skills, lack of impetuosity, and giver of good counsel.

The hardest form of passive-aggressive behavior to manage, because it is hard to spot and harder to stop, is two-facedness—smiling sweetly at a community member one minute, then destroying the member with malicious gossip when that member is elsewhere. The best way to deal with this problem is peer pressure; by creating an environment in which peers put a clamp on the gossipy behavior. Such a workplace must grow an environment founded on trust, caring, and a commitment to the higher mission of the organization. Leaders are those who help create and reinforce such an environment. Too many organizations are led by those who destroy it by listening to the gossip, sometimes actually seeking it out in the name of "gathering information for the annual review." Some supervisors with low self-esteem seek to be the hero-problem-solver and jump into the fray when they hear the tale of the gossip or the tattler. By doing so, they reinforce the passive-aggressive behavior and reward the termites who are eating the unit's foundation.

A further form of such malicious behavior is withholding information. Information that a co-worker could use to be effective is held back so the person will not be allowed to "look good." This clearly indicates a lack of teamwork, the absence of a spirit of collaboration, and a loss of dedication to the organization's mission. A consultant can show a work unit how to build a team, but no one can build a team except the team.

A final example—and there are dozens more—of counterproductive behavior is withholding energy. The animals had been doing this effectively ever since they discovered how the executive bonus program worked. They found they could put less than half of their available energy into achieving the mission before the supervisors gave them grief. This behavior does more to unite the workers against the managers than any other form. Once again, the solution is leadership that engages the workers in the mission of the organization.

Emerson was adept and forthright in addressing the issues as they came up, so passive-aggressive behavior was not a serious problem in the barn-yard until the merger. The arrogance and the unwillingness or inability of the race horses to do any "real" work caused major problems, and Emerson could do little but watch with great sadness. He had moral authority among the animals of the Firm, but the race horses did not even acknowledge his existence. After all, he couldn't even run! He had no position-authority or title since they closed down the training function, and those with titles or position-authority either chose not to take action, or they didn't know what to do. And they certainly would never ask advice of someone beneath them in the hierarchy. Those on the company's own payroll are rarely heard. If they were, consultants would starve.

The Pigs were aware that a problem existed, but they couldn't even give it a name other than "bad blood" between the race horses and all the other animals. This was a classic case of merging two disparate cultures without proactively implementing a carefully crafted culture management process. Maybe time will heal those wounds—maybe not. This is a business, not a church or a shrink's couch. They'll just have to tough it out.

When the productivity numbers began to slide, the Pigs relented and agreed to hire a consultant—not the owls this time. They had tried and failed. They were too "touchy-feely." This time, they agreed the Firm needed a consultant specializing in teambuilding, conflict management, group problem-solving and organizational effectiveness. They consulted the yellow pages, talked to animals in other firms, and even asked a few Humans for their opinions. They finally settled on a company run by a gray-haired muskrat and a smooth talking possum.

This company promised to deliver something called Total Quality Management, or, TQM for short—a system that would teach the lowest level of working animal how to measure their own output, find ways to improve that output, and monitor their progress using something called "statistical process control." By installing this system, the working animals would feel they have a stake in the outcomes, they would have a sense of ownership, and they would come up with the best solutions because they are the closest to the work. And, in the bargain, teamwork would be a happy byproduct, group decision-making would become a necessary skill, and they would necessarily become experts at conflict management.

This sounded like the solution to all the problems, and the Pigs signed a long-term high dollar contract. The silver-headed muskrat and the silver-tongued possum disappeared and were rarely seen again. Their sumptuous limousine was replaced by a big, yellow school bus loaded with squirrels—smart squirrels, mind you—they had MBA's—but squirrels with zero experience and none of the wise humility that comes from having hit a few of the potholes in the road of life.

The squirrels set to work quickly. They conducted classes in team leadership for all middle managers, mostly sheepdogs, but now and then a goat with long, sharp horns. These they turned into "mentors" and "coaches." Each of these mentors was given responsibility for a team of workers from a common functional area. They blessed the proceedings with their benevolent presence as the squirrels taught the workers how to identify and analyze a problem, gather data, consider a variety of possible alternative solutions, select one proposed solution using statistical tools, test that solution to see if it works, then move on to the next problem. Unfortunately, the new problem is often caused by the solution to the old one.

There were several problems with the TQM approach. First, it was not easy to get upper management to fully support it. They were reluctant to give up control of the decision making process. Second, there was no way they were ever going to get the race horses involved, let alone committed. They were too busy running around and looking good. They had no interest in sitting for long periods of time using their heads instead of their legs.

And third, the most problematic one—the working animals did not want to make the tough decisions and do all the analysis. What was in it for them? No increase in food, all their spare time being filled with sheets of statistics and analytical problems, and very few of their ideas ever get adopted and implemented by upper management. After all, upper management is paid to do this stuff, not them. All this does is give them more work to do, more headaches, making it impossible to just go back to their stalls at the end of the day, to relax, play with the kids, watch television and drink beer.

So, after a year and lots of bucks, the contract was cancelled and the Firm went back to "business as usual—back to the basics." The hierarchical structure prevailed, and the Pigs went back into the traditional boss mode. The animals stopped gathering and analyzing statistics, stopped making recommendations that were ignored. They became even more cynical than they were before the TQM consultants showed up.

Emerson felt that his time had come to speak out. He would await his opportunity. He was prepared.

CHAPTER TEN

Emerson's Pyramid

If you cannot work with love but only with distaste, it is better that you should leave your work and sit at the gate of the
temple and take alms from those who work with joy.

Kahlil Gibran

The Prophet

What do we live for, if it is not to make life less difficult to
each other?

George Eliot

Middlemarch

The Total Quality Management training was not a complete bust. One concept from the TQM training struck a responsive note in the hearts and minds
of the animals—that one could measure one's effectiveness by finding out
if the customer is pleased. "Customer satisfaction" became the new catch
phrase. A new consultant was hired, a young pony, but this one did not last
long. He got on everyone's nerves very quickly, especially when the animals
discovered he was a "one-trick pony." All he could talk about was identifying
your customers, both internal and external customers, and find out what

they want, what they do with what they get from you, and where are the gaps between the two.

"You know, we could be profitable and we could all enjoy a nice increase in our food allowance if we stopped hiring so many consultants," one hen observed sagely.

At the conclusion of one of these painful sessions, Emerson went to the chart pad and asked for permission to use it. Permission was granted, and all the animals leaned forward. Emerson had done this before, and they were eager to hear what he had to say.

With some effort, he drew a pyramid on the chart pad. He asked the assembly, "Do you agree that most organizations look like a pyramid?"

There was general assent, so the bull went on. "At the top of the pyramid sits the organization's most significant decision maker, the check signer—whatever his or her title might be. And down here at the bottom of the pyramid are the working animals that have the most direct contact with the customer. Their task is to please the customer so there will be repeat business and referrals."

Emerson looked around and read his audience to see if they were still with him. They were, so he went on: "Now, the customer is out here some

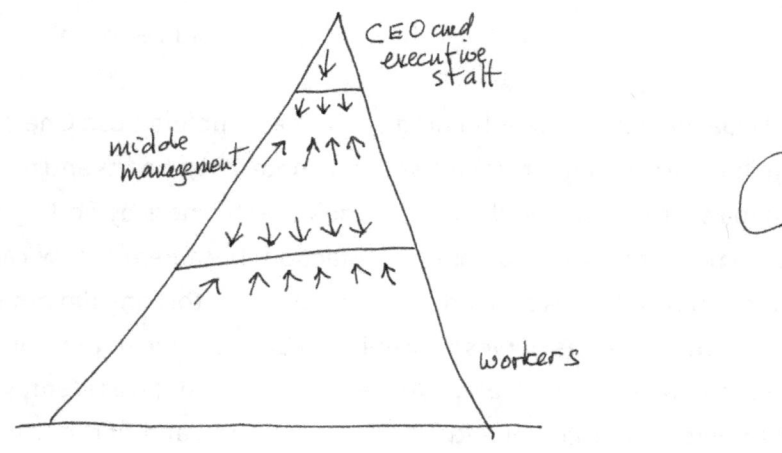

where . . ." and he drew a big letter "C" on the chart pad. "But the workers are not stupid. They know who writes the performance evaluations. They know who determines if the animal will get a pay increase, so who is the customer?"

Emerson looked around for a few seconds, then answered his own question.

"Not the cash-paying large C individual out here, but the supervisors of the working animals. In fact, the big C-customers are often a bother to the workers because they get in the way of pleasing the supervisors. Some of them even have the effrontery to complain about the quality of service or the rudeness of an employee to the Big Kahuna, and his or her displeasure rolls down through the pyramid and makes everyone messy. And, worst of all, it creates an adversarial relationship between supervisors and workers, and between workers and customers."

The animals looked at each other and nodded. It is true, they agreed, that the real customer is the boss who controls the welfare of each of them in his or her cloven feet.

Emerson went on. "The qualities of a pyramid include descriptors like 'big,' 'stable,' 'unmovable,' 'impervious to changes in the environment,' and 'full of dead people.'"

A chuckle rolled across the floor of the barn. They had been told too many times by the Pigs that the only good Human was a dead Human. Emerson was referring to the dead wood in middle management he had read about.

"So, to solve this problem," Emerson continued, "one of our astute consultant friends has suggested that we turn the pyramid upside down! With the bosses at the bottom, providing support to the workers who are at the top, serving the customers."

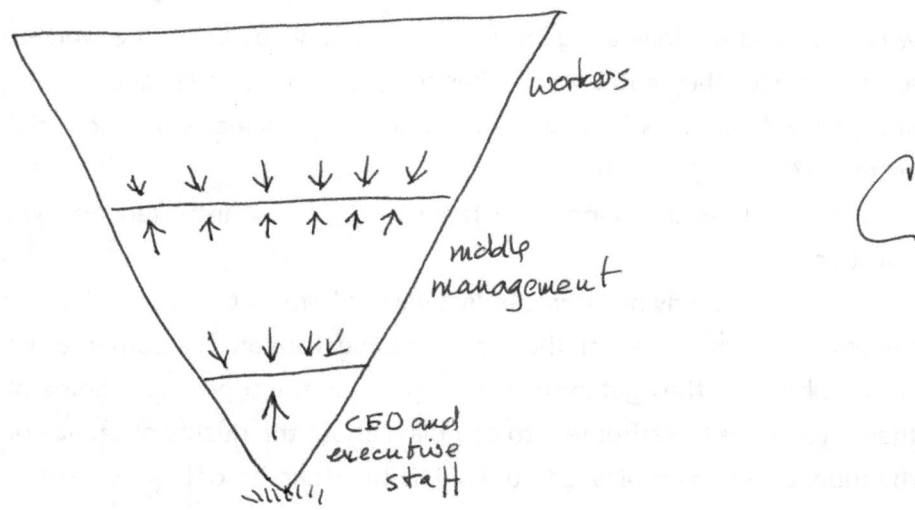

"The idea behind this pyramid is that workers are empowered by their bosses to serve the customer in whatever way it takes to make them happy."

Emerson paused for effect, then went on: "There are some serious flaws with this model. For starters, no one can empower anyone else, just as no one can change another animal against its will. A leader can create an environment in which an animal can choose to empower itself, but it cannot be mandated on another. One does not empower by memo or edict. Empowerment is an organic thing—it grows like a tree. It cannot be designed and assembled like a machine."

"Second fatal flaw: the folks who call the shots and sign the checks are at the bottom now, but they still call the shots and sign the checks. A benevolent dictator is still a dictator. A smiling tyrant is still a tyrant, and the animals know it. All they have really done is expose the workers to greater risk of hassle from both the customer and the supervisor. And it takes the average worker less than a heartbeat to sniff that one out."

"A final flaw: the pyramid is unstable, and the check signers will become impatient with it because they are worried about some not-so-smart worker giving away the farm to a crafty customer. The bottom line, for which all managers are held accountable, becomes very hard to control. Before long, management will say, 'To hell with this—it's back to the basics!' and the whole noble experiment goes down the tube."

"The qualities of this pyramid are, as I have already observed, instability. It remains impervious to the effects of the environment, it still cannot move anywhere, and while it is not full of dead people, it will collapse of its own internal contradictions."

"There is a third kind of pyramid—and this is not new. It has been tried and used successfully in many organizations. It looks like this," and Emerson drew the following diagram on the chart pad.

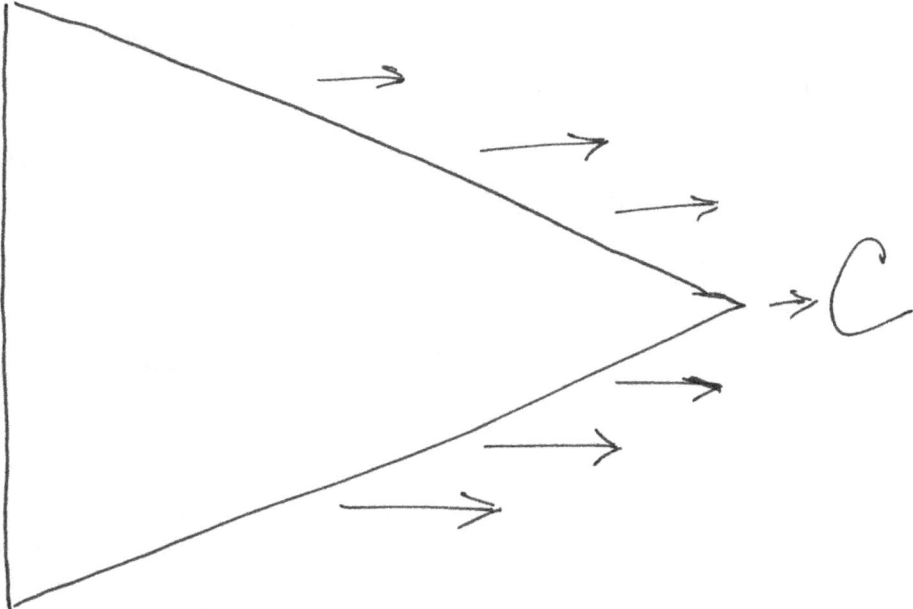

"You see," he intoned, "we have something that looks like a nose cone or an arrowhead. It is very responsive to its environment because it needs the wind currents to maintain stability. It also must move forward, or it will go straight down into the dirt. So right away we see that two of its qualities are responsiveness to its environment and the ability, the necessity, to move forward to maintain itself."

The animals began to get it. "So where is the boss and where are the workers? And who serves the customers? And where are they?"

Emerson drew on his diagram the location of the supervisors, whom called "resource providers," and the workers, called "implementers," showing how they worked interdependently to directly address the requirements of the customer.

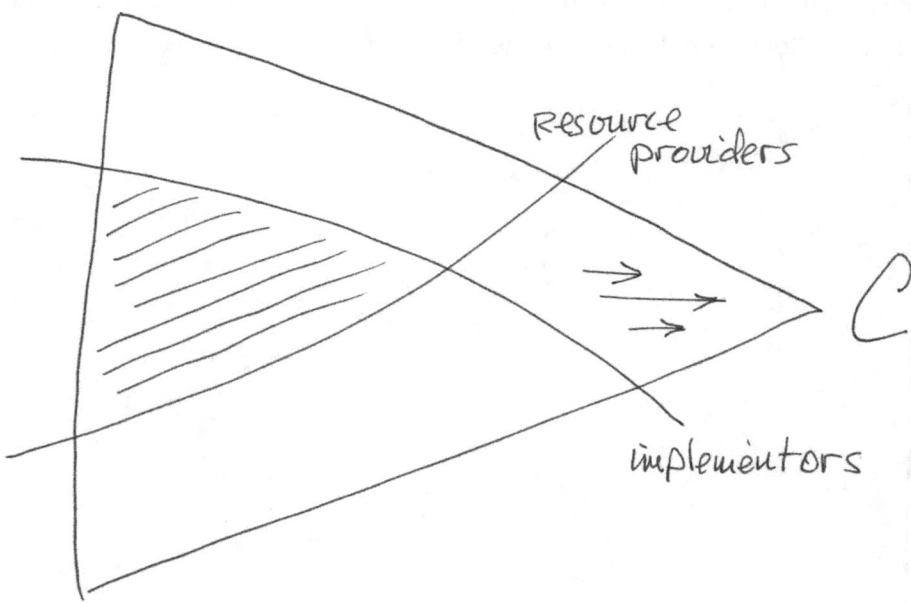

"You see, the ones who provide the resources cannot be successful without the cooperation of those who do the work, and *vice versa*. We need each other if we are going to please customers. So it makes no sense at all to make life more difficult for each other. As an American President said years ago, "Don't spit in the soup! We all have to eat."

"Is such an organization possible?" several of the animals asked.

"It's possible, but it's not easy. First, you need an organization comprised of people who are psychologically, emotionally, and spiritually healthy. They are not driven by greed or fear, but by healthy ambition, guided by the organization's mission. They are not workaholics, victims, or possessed of an entitlement mentality. They are willing to manage their egos for the good of the community, to submit to the authority of the mission—and by the way, the 'mission' and 'the bottom line' are not synonymous. All members of the organization must be committed to the mission. The bottom line guides and motivates upper management, because they have to report to the Board and the shareholders. They all must live by the Golden Rule, which, by the way, has been with us for thousands of years and is at the core of all the great world religions."

The animals sat in stunned silence. Why can't we do this here? What holds us back? Even the one-trick pony sat with mouth hanging open. Why not? Emerson, meanwhile, had quietly taken his seat while the animals talked in low tones. One by one, each animal slipped off to his or her sleeping place. Maybe a good night's sleep would show them how to put these ideas to work here—now—in this organization.

CHAPTER ELEVEN

A Change in Management

A wise man is informed by what is right. The inferior man is informed by what will pay.

Confucius

If work is a good thing, the rich would have it all and not let you do it.

Elmore Leonard

The next morning, the animals gathered in the barnyard for their daily pep talk, which would begin in a few moments. They talked quietly among themselves, seeming to find consensus that Emerson's ideas made sense—that we can implement them in our own organization without a porcine blessing, and the racehorses would not be able to do anything about it. They might even come to envy it and try to copy it.

Instead of the usual "power of positive thinking" and "we need you—you are our most important asset speech" by Squealer, a memo came to the assembled group, delivered by a sheepdog who was obviously shaken:

We are sad to announce that Mr. Napoleon the 13th, our revered and much-loved leader for so many years, has resigned from Animal Firm, effective yesterday. He has decided to consider other career options that night be available to him, and to spend more quality time with his family.

A new CEO will arrive in two weeks. In the meantime, Squealer will be acting CEO. There will be more information about the successor to our beloved Napoleon the 13th later today or early tomorrow. In the meantime, we wish Mr. Napoleon the 13th the best as he considers the many options that will obviously be opening up for him. Let us show our support and gratitude for him by falling in behind Squealer during this difficult time of transition.

There was no official information for the next week. By the time the announcement came forth, the animals had already heard via the rumor mill that the new CEO was a Bengal tiger, recruited from the nearest municipal zoo.

"A tiger!? What does a tiger know about farming? How does he regard farm animals as other than food?" The animals looked at Emerson, hoping for some comfort. Not surprisingly, Emerson had read about the human's fondness for the tiger—a creature of action, that gets results, that invigorates lackadaisical companies and lights a fire under their tails. And, they aren't reluctant to get rid of the deadwood. Emerson pondered, searching for the right words, to tell them the truth without terrifying them.

"To the humans," he finally began, "a tiger is the symbol of quick decisiveness and results-oriented action. The tiger is one who can spot a company's weaknesses and take corrective action, turning a weak company into a strong and profitable one. A tiger is a master of corporate transformation. A tiger won't need an army of consultants to gather data and devise stratagems. They operate on the basis of high trust in their own intuition, abundant self-confidence, and enormous egos."

"Does that mean we are in for a bloodbath?" asked one of the roosters.

"Well, 'bloodbath' is a very strong word. I'd say we are undoubtedly in for some major changes—and fast. But, you can't run a farm without animals." An ill-suppressed smile crawled across Emerson's face: "After all, you've heard our leaders often say that we are their most important asset." Someone in the back made a puking sound.

"All right. I'll be honest with you." (What had Emerson been doing up to that point—lying?) "We are in for some major changes, and, despite what we hear from the Pigs or what we read in the memos, the changes will not all be pleasant. Tigers like to make a big splash on their first day in a company. Their main task is to impress the Board with their penchant for action, whether or not it is carefully considered action. And tigers like to get results—any results—because that thrills investors. Better bad news in the business rags than no news at all."

The new CEO arrived before most of the animals were awake. He even beat the rooster to the punch. He had already made a number of decisions by the time a handful of very red-eyed Pigs came out the back door with an announcement for the waiting animals.

> Our new CEO has arrived and has assumed his responsibilities effective this morning. His name is Mack Yavelli, and he comes to us with years of experience as a "turnaround" specialist. He likes to be called 'Sir.' That's all the information we have for you now. We suggest you keep looking very busy for the rest of the day.

And they turned tail and trotted humbly back into the Firmhouse.

Emerson spoke first: "Mr. Yavelli has quite a reputation for 'transforming' companies. His nickname (no pun intended) is 'Ripsaw Nick.' And he has earned his reputation by taking no prisoners, getting the results the stockholders and board members want, and showing no remorse when he departs from the scene of the carnage."

Several animals whimpered. They had never heard Emerson use such mercilessly graphic language. The euphemisms and the understatements were absent. No doubt Emerson felt his time was short, that the new regime would quickly discover his expendability, and he would be looking for a new situation.

As anticipated, the fur and feathers soon began to fly. Reorganization directives came flying out the back door of the Firmhouse with increasing frequency, and the animals learned that a tiger's roar can make Pigs fly. Finally, Ripsaw Nick made an appearance, and that, combined with his demeanor, made quite an impact on the animals. In quick order, the following changes would be made:

- The racehorse stable would be sold off. The cost/benefit factor was not there. The horses cost too much to feed per head, and the groomers' and trainers' salaries were exorbitant.
- The goats and ducks would all be sent to "petting zoos." They did not produce enough marketable foodstuffs to justify a farm existence.
- There will be a reduction in force among the horses, especially among those that had been working at the racehorse stable. They will be sold to theme parks where they can pull carriages of tourists.
- The chickens, cows and sheep will be given strict production quotas. Those that don't make their quotas will be given separation packages.

There were a few other changes, but those were the most memorable and the most stunning. The positive thing about the tiger's whole speech: he did not end it with drivel about the animals being the firms' most important asset. He did say something to the effect that "a rising tide raises all boats." Emerson thought to himself, "True, assuming all the boats are seaworthy. Those that aren't remain on the bottom, stuck in the mud, soon to make for hazardous sailing for everyone."

No comment about plans for Emerson.

The changes were implemented with machine gun speed. Lifelong friends were separated without even a moment to wish each other well. As the goats, ducks and horses were loaded into the boxcars, one wondered if they would all end up in petting zoos or theme parks. None of them were ever heard from again.

The quotas went into effect immediately. Within a few weeks, a number of the animals were given "packages" giving them freedom to wander around the countryside looking for alternative employment. Each animal was given enough food for a week. In exchange, they were required to agree not to sue the Firm or to say anything negative about the Firm, the CEO or anyone in a supervisory role at the Firm. The released animals quietly cleaned out their stalls while a sheepdog watched to make sure nothing other than the animal's personal property went out the door. A terse announcement was made that "…so-and-so has decided to seek opportunities elsewhere. We are grateful for his/her contribution over the years, and wish him/her well."

Within four weeks, the Firm was half of its former size, while the workload and the quotas were undiminished. Even the Pigs' numbers were reduced. Squealer was no longer there. The tiger did not need a propaganda minister as much as he needed a yummy lunch of fresh pork. The animals that were still at the Firm were totally demoralized, walking around with their eyes to the ground, never speaking unless spoken to, and acting generally with great caution. Emerson was still there, but he never made another speech or answered any questions. He just shook his head sadly and moaned, and even then only when he sure no one else but trusted barnyard animals were present.

CHAPTER TWELVE

The Mind Benders

The average male gets his living by such depressing devices
that boredom becomes a sort of natural state to him.

H. L. Mencken
In Defense of Women

Who first invented work—and tied the free
And holy-day rejoicing spirit down
To the ever-haunting importunity
Of business, in the green fields, and
The town—To plough—loom—anvil—spade—
    And, oh, most sad,
To this dry drudgery of
The desk's dead wood?

Charles Lamb (1775 – 1834)

Not all went according to plan under the management of the tiger and his
cronies. More dramatic measures were called for, and the resourceful leadership was up to the challenge. When times are bad and the economy is going
through a rough patch, distract the folks with a few choice red herrings.

With the drop in the firm's "associate" headcount and the growing chasm between workers and management, a glaring leadership vacuum came into being that even Emerson could not fill. Nature abhors a vacuum, and organizations abhor a leadership vacuum. When good leaders do not step forward, the scoundrels and unprincipled opportunists will quickly offer their services, often hiding behind a feeble-minded talking head—a good-looking, glib "empty suit."

It was not long before a self-promoting religionist, using a small time television program slathered with generous applications of fear began scaring big bucks from the purses of the gullible. He became a prime-time nationwide media sensation by making irresponsible remarks and unsupportable accusations that were picked up by the major media outlets and bandied forth as the official viewpoints of the religion he claimed to espouse. He was nothing but a common weasel, but his slicked hair and tightly tailored suits gave him the appearance of prosperity.

He preached the gospel of prosperity—that if you were righteous, God would reward you with material plenty. He owned a private jet, several homes, and could afford to give millions to his favorite causes and political candidates. His sermons contained as many references to his personal political prejudices as to Holy Scripture, and he spent as much money to discredit those who opposed him as he spent supporting those who agreed with him, including ruthless dictators in developing countries. His daily television broadcast cost roughly $1 million an hour, and he concluded every telecast with a heart-rending plea to "save the country and save this program" by "reaching deeply into your savings accounts and your retirement nest eggs and send those dollars to me, the reverend Jerry Weasel, care of this television station."

He founded a college whose mission was to train preachers and politicians to carry on "the work:" to preach his version of the truth to the true believers and to promote legislation rooted in his political agenda. What he needed, while waiting for some of these young people to grow into positions of power, was a handful of office holders who would open doors for them. He found several. A famous elected official of a previous generation had been quoted as saying, "Money is the mother's milk of politics." If you had money to give away to ambitious politicians, you could quickly claim a loyal lap dog, or six, in the mahogany halls of power.

One such political lap dog was a cocker spaniel named Henry Bonniekins, who could be relied upon to clear all actions and proposals with the reverend before making any public statements. First, holy water from the Rev, then call a press conference.

Now, cockers in general are not intellectual giants, and rarely take a position on their own. They are consummate pleasers of their masters; they live for the next doggy milk bone, chew toy, or scritch behind the ears, to the affirming tune of "Good dog!" And what pleased the Reverend Weasel? Conformity; obedience; loyalty; the abolition of tolerance and diversity. The suppression, persecution, and public humiliation of any creature that challenged his beliefs or made him feel uncomfortable was certain.

The Reverend liked cocker spaniels, especially the puppies, because, after they were house-broken, they were pleasant to have around. They never questioned authority, and they were happiest when sitting quietly at the master's feet. If the Reverend had his way, all animals would be required to become cocker spaniels, or at least to act like cocker spaniels. Animals that refused to be a cocker spaniel were labeled unpatriotic, and not eligible to enter the paradise being prepared for worthy animals. Anti-dogs were vilified daily on "quack radio." Big-billed ducks, sounding more like barking dogs than any other animal, who were gifted with sarcasm and the ability to stretch the truth while maintaining a very straight face.

Congresspuppy Bonniekins has one over-riding passion that Reverend Weasel supported with energy and bucks—to name every unmovable object in the capital city after a revered former leader, President Tall King Head. An airport, a major congressional office building, and a major thoroughfare were not enough. Congresspuppy Bonniekins was writing legislation to name every one of the capitol city's 120,000 fire hydrants after President Head. Every dog walker in town would have to pause in reverent remembrance of the former leader as the canine expressed its appreciation for the existence of the monument.

The heavily gerrymandered congressional district of Congresspuppy Bonniekins included Animal Firm. Since the Firm was struggling, CEO Tiger thought it would be a good diversion to have Bonniekins, and maybe even Reverend Weasel, pay a visit, make a few fiery speeches, autograph some books and perhaps provide a photo-op for a few heavy donors. It would be good entertainment and take the minds of the animals off their aches and pains.

The CEO sent the invitation, along with a check, and the response was quick. Animal Firm was regarded by the Rev and the Congresspuppy as "a real mission field," full of non-dogs and anti-dogs in need of conversion. They arranged the visit for two months before the upcoming election, in plenty of time to encourage animals to register to vote. Mr. Tiger put up several campaign posters to announce the upcoming visit and to motivate all the animals to attend, except for the ones most likely to be critical of the candidate, ones who might perhaps be tempted to ask a challenging question. Those would have to be excluded.

The meeting was a rousing success. Many non-dogs and anti-dogs saw the light and changed their ways. There was one downer, however. Since the animals had no cash, they could purchase no souvenirs. All they could offer the visitors was a small share of their daily ration of feed from their troughs.

This event was a public relations disaster for the Reverend, the Congresspuppy and for Animal Firm. The cost of the visit was enough to put the Firm deeply into the red. The Board demanded accountability, but only after the appropriate government regulatory agencies began beating their tin drums.

CHAPTER THIRTEEN

The Acquisition

Figure it out. Work a lifetime to pay off a house. You finally own it, and there's no one to live in it.

Arthur Miller
Death of a Salesman

Term, holidays, term, holidays, till we leave school, and then work, work, work till we die.

C. S. Lewis
Surprised by Joy

The tiger lasted less than six months. It was discovered that he was cooking the books to make his results look impressive. He wasn't exactly doing anything illegal. He wasn't embezzling. He was just doing something unethical—concealing the truth from investors with intent to mislead. His actual results were not to be sneezed at. By reducing the size of the payroll, he had cut back on expenses so that, for the first time in years, the Firm was actually making a small profit, enabling the Board to pay off some long-term debt, and make the Firm attractive to a potential purchaser.

And it wasn't not long before the same came along. A conglomerate, Fiduciary Opportunism, Inc., comprised of six newspapers, a baseball team, an oil company, and part of a grocery chain, offered $3 over the current stock price, and the offer was quickly accepted. This made most of the Board members and a few of the Pigs very wealthy. The rest of the Pigs, and all the animals, got nothing except another period of anxious waiting.

The business rags took little notice of the purchase other than to note that the little company was recently managed by the notorious Ripsaw Nick, who was under investigation by Wall Street and a few other freelance attorneys. Fiduciary Opportunism, Inc., was famous for snapping up bigger fish than Animal Firm. One could wonder why they bothered, unless they were training some junior acquisitors.

Over the next few weeks, mysterious visitors with huge briefcases dropped in regularly at the Firmhouse. The Pigs had no information to offer about these visits. The communication between the Pigs and the other animals was never good, but it was now nonexistent—not even a memo now and then. Emerson, who maintained a low profile these days, had an idea that the new owners were going to do what takeover specialists so often do—split up the farm into marketable hunks, sell them off, and scuttle the rest. He didn't share this hunch with anyone else.

Emerson, sad to say, was once again correct. A great fleet of trucks drove up early one morning, some designed to carry animals and others carrying construction equipment. The cattle were separated from the sheep, and the Pigs—Oh! The Humility!—were loaded into separate trucks. They were all issued pagers—electronic leashes—and were told they were going to feed lots and breeding pens, where they would be fed as much as they could eat, but would be expected to work 80 hours a week while being paid for forty. They would have cubicles designed to keep them from exercising enough to lose weight, and to keep them from injuring one another in horse play.

The chickens were loaded into yet another truck. They were told they would enjoy the luxury of fourteen inch square cubicles, where they would have nothing to do all day but lay eggs. Some of the roosters were available for breeding, but most of them, along with any hens that didn't lay enough eggs, would be given other responsibilities to be revealed at a later time.

Before the trucks moved out of the yard toward their destinations, the construction equipment went to work. The bulldozers leveled the Firmhouse, the barn and all other outbuildings, then smashed the statues of the Founding Quadrapeds. A couple of workers put up a huge sign: "Future site of Harmony Firm Luxury Condos: 1 bedroom efficiencies starting at $350,000."

One truck remained to be loaded—a small pickup with open slat sideboards on the truck bed. A ramp went from the back of the truck to the ground, and Emerson was being prodded up the ramp. The tailgate was closed, and the truck drove off. A sign on its doors revealed its destination: Attila's Meats and Pet Food. Then, one by one, the other trucks moved toward the highway, leaving the dirt movers behind to finish their work.

* * *

CHAPTER FOURTEEN

Chaos

To get the whole world out of bed
And washed, and dressed, and warmed, and fed.
To work, and back to bed again,
Believe me . . . costs worlds of pain.

John Masefield
The Everlasting Mercy

Yonder, on the morning blink,
The sun is up, and so must I
To wash and dress and eat and drink
And look at things and talk and think
And work, and God knows why.

And often have I washed and dressed,
And what's to show for all my pain?
Let me lie abed and rest;
Ten thousand times I've done my best,
And all's to do again.

A. E. Housman

Emerson knew where he was going. He'd seen the truck before and had read the sign on the door. Strangely, he was not afraid, nor angry, but resigned to a certain fate. He wasn't sure about heaven or hell or an afterlife of any sort. He could look back over his life and say to himself, "I played the best I could with the cards that were dealt to me. I am prepared to face whatever lies ahead."

He found himself being prodded from the truck bed into a cold, dark room where other cattle were waiting. They all had an idea why they were there. Some were whimpering, others were muttering dark phrases about their captors, but most were just silent, unable to articulate their thoughts.

One of the cows recognized Emerson in the dim light. She tried to strike up a conversation, knowing that, even in this dark hour, Emerson would have something to say that was worth hearing.

"It's just not fair, Emerson! You work hard all your life, and when you are no longer of use, you get thrown onto the scrap heap."

Emerson thought carefully about how he should respond, if at all. Then it occurred to him that this was probably the safest place to say what he was really thinking. In the moments remaining in his life, he could say anything, and no one would be able to hold him accountable—unless, of course, there is an afterlife. Oh, well, what the heaven! Here goes.

"Fairness, my dear friend, is an arbitrary construct, put together by one of two kinds of creatures. The first are some people in power trying to justify whatever they are doing. The second is someone in our place, wishing that things were different, and calling on their own concept of fairness to justify, before some kind of cosmic justice, a course of action over which they have no control."

There was silence, as there always was after Emerson spoke. The silence was broken when a door opened, and one of the cattle was led out of the cement room by a uniformed Atilla's Meats worker. All sighed, knowing what was about to happen to the poor creature. Another door opened, and a member of their species joined them from the back of a truck.

"So, there is no such thing as fairness?"

"Only in our minds—in our wishful thinking."

"Then there is no justice on earth. There is no order in the universe. It's all chaos—an accident of evolution or the creation of a sadistic God."

Emerson let a few seconds tick by, then spoke slowly, choosing his words like a vegetarian scrutinizing a menu.

"There is justice. There is order. But most of us can't see it because we are too close to the fray."

"Explain—and quickly."

The door opened again, and another animal removed.

"I have never been in a ship at sea," Emerson began, "but from what I've read, there is nothing much more terrifying than being on the surface of the ocean during a high storm in a craft that seems to get smaller as the winds get fiercer."

"What could be more terrifying than being this room right now?"

"Well, if you think this room is all there is to existence, it would be terrifying indeed," Emerson responded, "but let me go on to make my point. I have been told by those who have been there that, even in a storm that has sailors saying their prayers, the fish twenty feet below the ocean's surface are not aware there is a storm in progress. All is tranquil and quiet where they are swimming."

"Furthermore, I have heard that, from an airplane thirty-five-thousand feet above the surface of the ocean, the surface looks placid, and the waves form a beautiful pattern that inspires poetry."

"And this leads you to conclude?"

"That we are a very small part of a big picture. We can't see the whole scene because we are clinging too tightly to what we think we know. We see ourselves as individuals, unique, deserving of special treatment, and not a part of a grand scheme of things that is larger than anyone of us. As we cling to what is closest to us, we think that is the only reality. And it doesn't behave the way we think it should. Of course it appears to us as chaos."

They could hear another truck drive up, and soon another cow joined them in the enclosure, which was beginning to smell a great deal like the feed lot from which some of them had come. After pausing long enough for the door to close and the new addition to find space, Emerson went on.

"I don't know how you get to see the whole cosmic scheme unless you use your imagination. None of us have been in an airplane, or twenty feet below the ocean's surface, but we can picture what it must be like by listening to those who have. What is philosophy, anyway, but the application of the imagination to the unknown."

The door opened, and the cow he had been addressing all along was pulled through. There were still two cows left of the group that was in the holding tank when Emerson first entered. All others had come after Emerson. From this he concluded that his number was three.

"My imagination tells me that what is closest to us, what is the most tangible, the most measurable, the most sensual, is the least real, the least significant ultimately. And yet, it is those very things that create the apparent chaos that makes our short lives so miserable. And our very society, our culture, our economy, is designed to make us want more, to make great sacrifices to get more of these inconsequential things. The merchants in our society have made addicts of us. They are the pushers. They have turned us into highly skilled professional consumers. It is our consuming that makes our economy appear to be prosperous. We have lost the ability to discern between the truly valuable and the cheap toys."

"Oh, shut up! Your wailing is making me sick!" one of the more recent arrivals muttered loudly.

"Mind your manners," Number Two said. "I want to hear what Emerson has to say."

"Oh! I apologize. I didn't realize we had the great Emerson in our company. If he is so smart, how did he end up in here with us?"

"Because life isn't about fairness," Number Two intoned. "Sometimes the dragon wins, the handsome knight in shining armor gets splattered all over the landscape, and the fair damsel remains in distress. And that's just the way it is. The universe doesn't revolve around us. We are all part of the ongoing story. We play our part as best we can, trying to make life less difficult for each other, hoping to leave the world in better shape than it was when we got here, because that's our nature. We have to be carefully taught to be otherwise."

"And who will hold us accountable?"

"Well, it sure won't be the stockholders or the board members or even our immediate supervisor when we were back at the firm," retorted Number Two.

The door opened, and Number Two became Number One.

Emerson spoke after a long silence.

"I have become convinced that, beneath the chaos we perceive and mistake for reality, there is a benign, perhaps even a nurturing, order that keeps the chaos within bounds. Most of the chaos we observe is of our own making, either because of our self-seeking or our naiveté. Some of it is provided by nature— earthquakes, floods, hurricanes—but it is not chaos until we declare it to be chaos. It's just natural, until it messes up something we value. Then it is a nuisance that gives rise to the insurance industry,"

"Emerson," cried Number One as the door opened, "will I see you on the other side?"

"I don't know. I hope so!"

And Emerson became Number One.

There wasn't anything left to say. All to do now was just wait. Silence prevailed except for the sound of sighs and an occasional whimper. The room somehow did not seem cold any more, possibly because of the body heat of animals packed closely together. The animals all touched each other. Since words didn't work, this was a way to communicate their love for each other.

The door opened, and Emerson was led out into a very bright white light.

THE END?

For all our days pass away under your wrath; our years come to an end like a sigh. The days of our life are seventy years, or perhaps eighty, if we are strong; even then their span is only toil and trouble; they are soon gone and we fly away.... So teach us to count our days, that we may gain a wise heart.

Moses: from the 90th Psalm